AF324839

Leeladhar Jagoori

What of the Earth Was Saved

translated from Hindi by Matt Reeck

What of the Earth Was Saved
Copyright © Leeladhar Jagoori, 2024
English translation copyright © Matt Reeck, 2024
Introduction copyright © Matt Reeck, 2024

Originally published as *Bachi hui prithvi*
by Rajkamal Prakashan in New Delhi, 1977

First Edition, First Printing, 2024
ISBN 978-1-954218-20-8

World Poetry Books
New York, NY
www.worldpoetrybooks.com

Distributed in the US by SPD/Small Press Distribution
www.spdbooks.org

Distributed in the UK and Europe by Turnaround Publisher Services
www.turnaround-uk.com

Library of Congress Control Number: 2024930193

Cover design by Andrew Bourne
Typesetting by Don't Look Now
Printed in Lithuania by BALTO Print

World Poetry Books publishes exceptional translations of poetry from a broad
range of languages and traditions, bringing the work of modern masters,
emerging voices, and pioneering innovators from around the world to English-
language readers in affordable trade editions. Founded in 2017, World Poetry
Books is a 501(c)(3) nonprofit and charitable organization based in New York City
and affiliated with the Humanities Institute and the Translation Program at the
University of Connecticut (Storrs).

Contents

Introduction

THE HINDI POET LEELADHAR JAGOORI was born on July 1, 1940, in a village near the headwaters of the Ganges River in the Himalaya Mountains. Misfortune shaped his early life. Jagoori's family were Brahmin, but they were too poor to effectively farm their land. His mother died of smallpox when he was five years old. He was beaten by his father. At eleven years old, he ran away from home without any money, eventually settling in a village in Rajasthan. At 17, he enlisted in the Indian Army, then went AWOL five years later during the Sino-Indian War of 1962, an act for which he was court-martialed. It was his poetry that saved him: in a 2015 national television interview with talk show host Jasleen Vohra, Jagoori described the frank letter he wrote at the time to Minister of Defense V. K. Krishna Menon, stating that he could perform better "service" to the country by writing poetry than by firing guns. Menon agreed, and his court-martial was avoided.

Jagoori had begun writing poetry in 1960. His first poems were folk songs in his first language, Garhwali, a language of over 2.5 million speakers in the northern Indian state of Uttarakhand, Jagoori's home state. He says now that he stopped writing these songs both because he was increasingly distant from the context in which they would have meaning and because he was not good at performing them. After being discharged from the army, he traveled to the cities of Eastern Uttar Pradesh, seeking patronage from established Hindi poets. He enrolled at Banaras Hindu University in Varanasi to earn an MA in Hindi literature, and in 1964, under the caste name Leeladhar Sharma, published his first volume of poetry.

Jagoori has acknowledged the difficulties of his early life, but he insists that his biography is not unusual: he knew "hundreds" if not "thousands" of people like himself—ordinary citizens who had to undergo periods of trial and tribulation in the newly independent India before finding their footing in the world. In part as a gesture toward this fact, he had changed his name to Leeladhar Jagoori by the time his second volume of poetry, *The Play Is Underway* [नाटक जारी है] was published in 1972. Jagoori was the name by which local villagers had identified his family during his childhood, and he no longer wanted to present himself so obviously through the template of caste, which had little to do with his experiences in life.

For Jagoori, the impact of external circumstances on the formation of personality is undeniable, and it's likely that his sense of social and political engagement developed from his experiences in the 1960s. He has written about how desperate many young adults felt in the second full decade of Indian independence, how "the new generation that came into consciousness in the days after Independence" had in many cases been pushed to "the brink," contemplating suicide. Their lives seemed "meaningless," and they "saw history, tradition, and the world around them as nothing more than another age of misery." The struggles of many people in the young nation continued in the 1970s, a volatile, violent decade, which included the 21-month period called the Emergency (1975–77), when Prime Minister Indira Gandhi, a democratically elected leader (and the daughter of the first Indian Prime Minister Jawaharlal Nehru), instituted authoritarian rule. She suspended civil rights, censured the press, conducted mass sterilization campaigns, and violently "cleared" slums with little forewarning and no resettlement plans for the displaced.

In an interview from February 2023, Jagoori emphasized that, instead of writing poetry in the fashion of the times, his effort has always been to focus on "having something to say." His fifth poetry collection, *What of the Earth Was Saved*, was his first to be published after the end of the Emergency. The volume's antiauthoritarian position is evident in both obvious and subtle ways. Several of the poems speak directly to the suppression of civil liberties during the Emergency. "Inter-Indian Mail," for example, effectively "outs" the surveillance state and its desire to pry into private lives. "Baldev Kathik" depicts the social divide between haves and have-nots, with those living in the Himalaya Mountains figuring as second-class citizens, without equal access to food and medicine. The poem also deals with the subject of police brutality, a form of oppression that devastates both its victim and its agent: a poor mountain-village man arrested for stealing food rations to feed his hungry family, and the poem's title character, a subaltern police officer, who goes insane in response to the violence he is compelled to commit.

Jagoori's regional consciousness and environmentalism seem to anticipate the recent trend of eco-poetry. India, of course, has a long history of ecological consciousness: Uttarakhand saw, in 1973, the birth of the Chipko Movement, a grassroots ecological movement formed to counteract development and protest the Indian government's forest resource management decisions. The consciousness of resistance and local autonomy is manifest through his poetry's environmental or place-based language and imagery pulled from the mountains. Birds feature prominently throughout. In "Baldev Kathik," crows become symbols of the unwitting victims of state violence. That poem ends with the haunting suggestion that when the police, or other authoritarian enforcers of the state's will, open fire in the future, "it won't be crows that die," but people.

Other poems evoke the social milieu of impoverished mountain communities via the emotional and geographically specific language characteristic of Jagoori's poetry. "The Old Woman's Song of Herself as a Young Girl," for instance, voices the memories of a woman looking back on her childhood in the countryside, where "fireflies enticed [her] back out" every evening after she returned home. The speaker in "The Waiting Place" stands "on the mountain peak / of music / hundreds of years old." His world is one filled "with the scent of / freshly dug-up earth." The long narrative poem "The Tale of Two Clever Boys," which is redolent of Hindi folk tales, tells the story of two young boys, Babaloo and Pappu, out wandering the mountain roads in the countryside, playing make-believe, and arguing playfully with each other.

Jagoori's foregrounding of antiauthoritarianism and regional consciousness and his self-identification with the trials and travails of the mountain poor make him unique among Hindi poets of the 1970s, and of postcolonial India in general. Yet, far from being a spokesman for certain ideological positions, he writes poetry from an individualistic stance in keeping with his creative desire to invent across a broad range of free-verse forms. While this is only one of his five poetry volumes written in the 1970s, it is emblematic of his response to that decade's social struggles, just as it showcases the delightful variety of his poetic expression.

MY FULBRIGHT YEAR IN INDIA proved shorter than intended. While the rest of my cohort was already in India as 9/11 unfolded on international news, I was still in Manhattan, Kansas, waiting for my institutional affiliation to be approved by the Kendriya Hindi Sansthan (Central Hindi Institute). My eventual arrival coincided with another terrorist attack. On December 13, 2001, five terrorists drove a car into the Indian House of Parliament while I was just a few miles away, walking the streets of Old Delhi. Soon afterward, I found a flat in the Delhi Development Authority compound near the Shri Aurobindo Ashram in Adchini, across the street from the institute. My fellowship was, like me, mixed genre, with mixed designs: not only was I to continue studying Hindi, but I was also to write poetry. Outside of occasional meetings with a Hindi professor, the rest of my time was more or less unstructured. In the mornings, I would bike over to Jawaharlal Nehru University, leave my bike by the East Gate, and wander through the bushes with the peacocks toward the dirt track, where I would jog. At least once a week, I would travel by bus to central Delhi to print poems at the American Center Library and buy Hindi books in the shops on Asaf Ali Road near Daryaganj, the book-selling neighborhood at the gates to Old Delhi. It was on one of these trips in spring 2002 that a bookseller recommended a book by Leeladhar Jagoori, originally published in 1977 and reprinted several times since. A bird perched on barbed wire under the book's evocative title, *Bachi hui prithvi*, literally, the "saved," or "remaining," "earth." I took it back to my apartment.

Skip forward to the COVID summer of 2020. I'm sitting on the couch at home looking at my bookshelves, books stacked two deep on their sides. A book catches my eye—the bird on the barbed wire. Reading it for the first time in nearly twenty years, I'm struck by how the poems feel like prophesies about contemporary American problems: emergent authoritarianism, the strained environment, and a fragmentation of social relations across divides, most notably between the rural and urban.

Soon after, I start looking online for Jagoori's email contact. By late August, I find it by way of an obscure Hindi literature website, and quickly we're talking via WhatsApp, and he grants me permission to translate the book. Now I am struck by the symmetry of these events: I purchased the book a quarter century after its original publication, and now, after nearly a quarter century since its purchase, I have the chance to publish its translation in English.

Matt Reeck, January 2024

बची हुई पृथ्वी

What of the Earth Was Saved

अपने जन्म से ३५ वर्ष और आगे चलकर
मिट्टी का हिस्सा बनने से पहले
वह कोख थी
कभी जिसकी वजह से मैं संसार में आया
जिसका नाम शाकम्बरी था
उस अनाथ लड़की को

35 years after her birth and before
she would be folded back into the earth
she was that womb
that brought me into the world
whose name was Shakambari

—this is
for that orphaned girl

मौत के शोर और जीवन के सन्नाटे में
गौर से देखो
जहाँ पर किताबों के फाटक बंद होते हैं
दैनिक दुख की गूँज के रू-ब-रू
शब्द
समय और हवा-पानी
इन पर हमारे नाम के गाँज हैं

look carefully at the noise of death
and the calm of life
where the gateway of books is closed
to face the echoes of our daily grief
words
time and nature
are all we have

आलोचक से

जिन्होंने देखा और पाया नहीं
जहाँ मैं था
वर्जित इलाके में
वे किसी बदनाम शब्द को
मार रहे थे
जिसे मैं बदल नहीं सका

बहुत-से जो मुझे देख रहे हैं
पहले से
वे अगर देख लें तो इंकार कर दें
जो परसों तक सबने किया
उसके विरुद्ध एक नया इन्कार ।

To the Critic

those who looked but didn't find
where I was
deep in the countryside
they were saying
such awful things about
what I couldn't change

many of those looking at me
if they ever really look
reject at once
what everyone did until till two days ago
gets rejected too

अंतर्देशीय

इस पत्र के भीतर कुछ न रखिए
न अपने विचार
न अपनी यादें
इस पत्र के भीतर कुछ न रखिए

न अपने संबंधों की छाप
न दुःख, न शिकायतें
न अगली मुलाकात का वादा
न संत्रामक बीमारियां
न पारिवारिक प्रलाप
न अपने हस्ताक्षर
वरना ये पत्र पकड़ा जा सकता है
इस पत्र के भीतर कुछ न रखिए

क्योंकि जिनका 'ठिकाना' नहीं
वे असहाय
सबसे ज़्यादा संदिग्ध हैं
बाहर एक ओर किसी पानेवाले का
नाम और पता
दूसरी ओर किसी भेजनेवाले का
ज़रूर हो

समाचार खुद हिफाज़त चाहते हैं
इस पत्र के भीतर कुछ न रखिए

भेजनेवाला जानता है
क्या नहीं लिखा गया
क्यों नहीं लिखा गया
पढ़नेवाला जानता है

कोरा
वह भी बाँच लेगा
एक भी आखर

Inter-India Mail

don't put anything in this letter
not your thoughts
not your memories
don't put anything in this letter

nothing about your friends
no sadness
no complaints
no promise to get together
no news of illnesses
no family gossip
not your signature
or else this letter will be seized
don't put anything in this letter

because the homeless
draw the most suspicion
here on the envelope
the recipient's name and address
and there the sender's

news wants to be safe too
so don't put any in this letter

the sender knows
what wasn't written
why it wasn't written
the reader knows

a blank page
will be scoured as well
a single
incomplete syllable

जिसके हिस्से नहीं आया
इस पत्र के भीतर कुछ न रखिए

न कोई विस्फोटक शब्द
न बच्चा पैदा होने की खबर
न कोई आकस्मिक मृत्यु
न बम
न कोई वाजिब तर्क
न नये साल की बधाई
न तलाक का इरादा
इस पत्र के भीतर कुछ न रखिए

सारा मुद्दा
सारा पत्र
पोस्टमैन का रक्तहीन चेहरा है
जो रोज़ गाँजा जा रहा है
और जिसे
शाम को वह जमा भी नहीं कर सकता ।

don't put anything in this letter

no incendiary word
no news of a child's birth
no accidental death
no bomb
no reasonable logic
no wishes for the new year
no plans for divorce
don't put anything in this letter

the entire meaning
the entire letter
is the mailman's face
that during the day
grows more and more pale
and by nightfall
is a bloodless mask

चिड़िया-१

उसने कभी नहीं सोचा कि मेरा नाम चिड़िया है
वो
जो घोड़े की नसों में फँसी हुई
घोड़े की आँख से आकाश देखती है
और उड़ जाना चाहती है

वो
जो आदमी की नसों में उड़ान मारती
घोड़े में उड़ान मारती चिड़िया को देखती है
और गुत्थम-गुत्था हो जाना चाहती है
उसने कभी नहीं सोचा कि मेरा नाम चिड़िया है

लेकिन घोड़ा और आदमी
हरी घास से पटी हुई पृथ्वी ढूँढ रहे हैं
जो घोड़े से ज़्यादा दौड़ती है
और चिड़िया से ज़्यादा उड़ती है

जिसका एक डैना सागर
दूसरा पहाड़ हो
जंगल जिसके रोएँ हों
शब्दों में उगने का शोर हो
और खामोशी में घास की खुशबू हो
(उस घास की खुशबू)
जो समझती है कि मुझसे पहले
कोई घास नहीं उगी थी
(इतनी नयी)

दाना-पानीवाली ऐसी पृथ्वी पर
आदमी बार-बार
घोड़े पर सवार होकर
उस चिड़िया की खोज में निकलता है
जो पंख मारती चिड़िया की नसों में फँसी है

The Bird (I)

she never thought *my name is Bird*
she
who is trapped inside the horse's veins
who sees the sky from the horse's eyes
and wants to fly

she
who courses through the man's veins
who sees the bird
trapped inside the horse
and wants to wrestle and fight
she never thought *my name is Bird*

but horse and man
are looking for a world flush with green grass
that runs further than a horse
that flies further than a bird

whose one wing is the ocean
and whose other is the mountain
whose body hairs are the forests
where the sound of growing comes in words
where the sweet smell of grass lies in silence
(the sweetness of that grass)
the grass that thinks that
there was never grass before
(the world is that new)

on an earth of seeds and water
the man gets on the horse
time after time
and goes out searching for that bird

आदमी के भीतर जो चिड़िया है
घोड़े के भीतर जो चिड़िया है
बिजली जिस पर गिरेगी
उस किसी एक पेड़ से
बचना चाहती है

आकाश में पृथ्वी पर
अँधेरा है,
शब्दों की
नावें
अँधेरे में
पाल की जगह
जिन पर सन्नाटा है
एक ऐसा सन्नाटा
घोड़े का भूत जिसमें
घोड़े पर सवार
आदमी का भूत
आदमी पर
और चिड़िया का भूत चिड़िया पर सवार है

मगर जिसने कभी नहीं सोचा
कि मैं चिड़िया का भूत हूँ
या कि उदाहरण के लिए मेरा नाम चिड़िया है
उसने कभी नहीं सोचा ।

beating its wings trapped
inside the veins of the bird

the bird inside the man
the bird inside the horse
wants to escape
the tree
where the lightning will strike

in the sky
on earth
there's darkness
the boats
of words
in the darkness
on the mound
are wrapped in stillness

a stillness like
when the ghost of the horse
is riding the horse
the ghost of the man
is riding the man
and the ghost of the bird is riding the bird

but she was the one
who never thought
I am the ghost of the bird
or if you prefer
my name is Bird

अन्तिम शिखर पर

इस जगह । इस रंग पर
नहीं होना चाहिए अन्त

ओ मेरे अन्तरंग !
कहीं कैद होना पड़े
कहीं गुम
भीतर-ही-भीतर
अन्तिम शिखर पर उगने के लिए
मगर वैसे नहीं चढ़ना है
जैसे कि रंग

उड़ान ढूँढोगे
तो पक्ष में पाओगे
पर वैसे नहीं उड़ना है जैसे कि रंग

मैं ऐसा चाहता हूँ ओ मेरे अन्तरंग !
कि सैंकड़ों दिनों से मुँदी हुई
कई हज़ार आँखें
बाहर के संसार में खोल दूँ

जैसे कि एक अखरोट ज़मीन में
दबा दूँ
तो वह उगे
पत्थर दबा दूँ तो वह उगे
आत्मा की रेत से मज़बूत तना लेकर

ओ मेरे अन्तरंग !
अखरोट पर फूल
और पत्थर पर चूना खिले
तो सबके घर पोत दूँ
जिन्हें मकानों ने खोंस रखा है

The Last Pinnacle

this place | this feeling
shouldn't be the end

O my soul!
somewhere a prison
somewhere desolation
inside the inside
to grow on the last peak
but nothing grows stronger
the way emotions do

you will search for flight
and find wings
but nothing soars
the way emotions do

O my soul!
I want to make thousands of eyes
asleep for hundreds of days
open and see the world

if I were to bury a walnut
it would grow
if I were to bury a stone it would grow
a strong trunk emerging from the soul's sand

O my soul!
if flowers bloom on the walnut tree
and lime slake appears on stones
I will whitewash all the homes
crammed inside the buildings

और जिनमें लोग इस तरह रहते हैं
जैसे पेटी में औज़ार

क्योंकि चमक वही ठीक है
ओ मेरे अन्तरंग !
जिससे किसी को रास्ता दिखे ।

where people live
like tools in a satchel

because O my soul!
the resplendence is good
that shows someone the way

आऊँगा

नये अनाज की खुशबू का पुल पार करके
मैं तुम्हारे पास आऊँगा
ज्यों ही तुम मेरे शब्दों के पास आओगे

मैं तुम्हारे पास आऊँगा
जैसे बादल
पहाड़ की चोटी के पास आता है
और लिपट जाता है
जिसे वे ही देख पाते हैं
जिनकी गरदनें उठी हुई हों

मैं वहाँ तुम्हारे दिमाग में
जहाँ एक मरुस्थल है
आना चाहता हूँ

मैं आऊँगा
मगर उस तरह नहीं
बर्बर लोग जैसे कि पास आते हैं
उस तरह भी नहीं
गोली जैसे कि निशाने पर लगती है

मैं आऊँगा
आऊँगा तो उस तरह
जैसे कि हारे हुए
थके हुए में दम आता है ।

I'll Come to You

crossing the bridge of the fresh grain's sweet scent
I'll come to you
just as soon as you accept my words

I'll come to you
like the cloud
that approaches the mountain summit
and swallows it
only those whose heads are raised
will be able to see it

I want to come to the desert
inside your mind

I'll come
but not like barbarians do
and not like a bullet
striking its target

I'll come
I'll come like new life
comes to a beaten-down
exhausted soul

तथाकथित महान लोग

तथाकथित महान लोग रात का क्या करते हैं ?

महान लोग रात को लबादे की तरह नहीं ओढ़ते
जैसे कि कैदी ओढ़ते हैं
रात उनके लिए
दिन-भर के कुकर्मों पर पड़ा हुआ पर्दा है
रात के सामने वे झुके हुए होते हैं
क्योंकि उनके कहने से
न वह गिरती है न उठती है

रात हरेक को प्रभावित करती है
कुछ घाव दिखते नहीं
केवल दर्द करते हैं
जो कहीं नहीं छिप सकते
उन्हें रात छिपा देती है

नंगे ;
अँधेरे को कपड़े की तरह लपेट लेते हैं
ढके हुए
पूरे नंगे हो जाते हैं
रात हरेक को प्रभावित करती है

कुछ महान लोग
दिन-भर रात का इन्तज़ार करते हैं
ताकि वे अपने ढोंग से
छुटकारा पा सकें

कुछ महान लोग रात के कपड़े बदलते हैं
और फिर से महान होने के लिए
सुबह का इन्तज़ार करते हैं

भूख की ज़रूरत से
ज़्यादा

"Important" People

what do so-called important people do at night?

important people don't cover themselves at night
like prisoners do
for them night
is camouflage for the sins of the day
they worship the night
because it doesn't come and go
on their command

night holds sway over everyone
no wounds are visible
though the pain persists
the pain that can't be hidden
that only night can hide

the naked
cloak the darkness
the hidden
are stripped nude
night holds sway over all

some important people
wait all day for night to come
to escape
their hypocrisy

some important people change the night's clothes
in order to be important again
they await the morning

a need
greater than hunger

तथाकथित महान लोग रात का क्या करते हैं ?

भूख से ज़्यादा
उनके घरों में जो भोजन घुस आया है
कुछ महान लोग उसके सड़ने को सूँघते हैं
और अपने ही कपड़ों को
अपने ही शरीर पर
गन्दा होते हुए देखते हैं

कुछ महान लोग सोचते हैं कि रात हो
इतनी लम्बी रात हो
एक लम्बी और साधारण ज़िन्दगी के लिए
कि जितनी लम्बी कोई रात नहीं हो सकती

दिन को उलटने के लिए
वे रात का इन्तज़ार करते हैं
और उसकी गलियों-जैसी चौड़ी नसों में
आवाज़ करते हुए
बिल्ले की तरह दौड़ना चाहते हैं
वे रात के काले ख़ून में तैरना चाहते हैं

कुछ महान लोगों के लिए
अपना चेहरा-जैसी चीज़
एक ग़लत-फहमी है
आईने में भी इनका चेहरा देख पाना
एक पागलपन है
उनके लिए अपना चेहरा लगभग अफ़वाह है

ऐसे महान लोग दिन-भर
अपने पैर देखने को तरस जाते हैं
जिन्हें कुछ लोग
जूतों के अन्दर घुसकर छूते हैं

क्योंकि जिनके साथ महान व्यवहार करते हैं
वे या तो दूसरे चेहरे होते हैं
या केवल काग़ज़

what do so-called important people do at night?

greater than hunger
some important people
luxuriate in the scent of their rotting food
they look to see their clothes
they wear grow soiled

some important people think
if there were a night
a night just so long
for a long and simple life
they think that no such night is possible

to reverse the day
they wait for night
and inside its protruding veins
they shout
and want to scamper like a cat
they want to swim in the night's black blood

for some important people
their face-like thing
is a misunderstanding
to look at their faces in the mirror
is madness
for them their faces are rumors

all day long
some important people
long to see their feet
that people touch
having entered their shoes

because the people with whom
important people come into contact

ऐसी रात को महान लोग जब अपने नंगे पैर देखते हैं
उन्हें अचानक एक झूठा यकीन होता है
कि हमारा कोई चेहरा भी होगा

वह चेहरा
जो न आफिस में होता है
न आईने में
वह चेहरा
जो उनके चेहरे में कभी नहीं होता
वे उस चेहरे के लिए रोते हैं
और अपनी मौत के डर से
बातचीत करते हुए
रात-भर खुद से घृणा करते हैं
सुई के छेद में डोरा
जो कुछ महान लोग
दिन को नहीं डाल सकते
वे रात का एक-एक बाल उखाड़ रहे हैं

उनकी सुबह
टूटे हुए बटनों के मुआवजे से शुरू होती है
उनकी सुबह
ढकने और छिपाने से शुरू होती है

दूसरी तरह से
ये लगभग लड़ाई का ऐलान है
कि तथाकथित महान लोग रात का क्या करते हैं ?

are either other faces or paper people

on nights when important people
look at their naked feet
suddenly a misplaced wish crosses their minds
that they too will have a face one day

that face
not found at the office
or in the mirror
that face
that is never their face
they cry for that face
and fearing their death
they talk through the night
hating themselves
some important people
are teasing apart the night's thread
fiber by fiber
that they failed to fit
through the eye of the needle
during the day

their morning
starts in exchange for broken buttons
their morning
starts with suppressing and hiding

or in other words
this is an announcement of conflict
what is it that so-called important people do at night?

इन्तज़ार की जगह

आज के संगीत की सीढ़ियाँ
आकाश में
कल के पत्तों से ढक दी हैं
इनसे होकर उतरना

मैं यहाँ हूँ
सैकड़ों वर्ष पुराने संगीत की
चट्टान पर

ताज़ा खोदी हुई
मिट्टी की गन्ध से भरी
आस-पास मेरी वर्तमान पृथ्वी है
कोख का
सारा कोयला दहकाये हुए ।

The Waiting Place

in the sky
the stairs of today's music
are covered with tomorrow's leaves
that we must descend

I am here
on the mountain peak
of music
hundreds of years old

the world today
is filled with the scent of
freshly dug-up earth
shaking each coal free
from the womb

तुम सुबह हो

दस लाख दिन
और दस लाख रातों के पार
एक लम्बे दिन की जड़ में
तुम एक सुबह हो

तुम्हारा चेहरा उस दिन का
सबसे बड़ा आश्चर्य है
मेरे लौट आने की
जिस दिन तुम्हें अन्तिम इच्छा है

ये दोनों
अलग-अलग दिशाएँ हैं
मेरा कहीं होना
और मेरा लौट आना

इन दोनों दिशाओं के बीच
गुज़रे दिनों और लापता रातों का
वो ख़्वाब है
जिसकी वजह से
दस लाख दिन और उतनी ही रातों के पार
तुम एक सुबह हो

एक ऐसी सुबह
जिसमें
बच्चे नहा रहे होंगे
नहा चुकी औरतों के
नहाये हुए बाल
चारों ओर एक जाल
एक रंग फैलायेंगे

और में उस मकड़े की तरह
अपने चमकते हुए सूत पहचानूँगा,
दस लाख दिन और रातों के पार

You Are the Morning

after one million days
and one million nights
at the start of a long day
you are the morning

the look on your face
is the largest surprise
on that day when your last wish
is my return

these signs
are not the same
my being somewhere else
and my return

between these two spaces
is the dream
of past days and forgotten nights
and when you wake
on the other side of a million days and nights
you are the morning

a morning
with bathing kids
and the clean hair of bathing women
casts a net
a mood all around

and like a spider
I will recognize my glistening thread
when after one million days and nights
will think about that time
and what else I could say to you

जिसके बारे में सोचूँगा
कि तुमसे और क्या कहना है

तुम्हारे अनोखे उजाले में
कई मिटे हुए चेहरे
एकदम चमक उठेंगे
कई पानी से भरे
खेत
धान को हृदय से उगाते
पनप उठेंगे

आटे में थोड़े-से नमक की तरह
तुम्हारी याद
मुझे स्वाद से भर देगी

घूमती हुई पृथ्वी के होंठों पर
दस लाख दिन
और दस लाख रातों के पार
ज़रूर कुछ नये शब्द मँडरा रहे होंगे
एक लम्बे दिन की जड़ में
जहाँ तुम एक सुबह हो
फिर से एक छोटी-सी
सुलगती हुई सुबह ।

in your special light
rubbed-out faces
will glisten and shine
crops will grow luxuriantly
from the hearts
of a row of well-watered fields

like a little salt mixed in flour
memories of you will
whet my appetite

on the spinning earth's lips
after crossing one million days
and one million nights
some new words will hover overhead
at the start of a long day
where you are the morning
a small smoldering morning once again

कायाकल्प

हरेक को संशय या कि संशय है
क्योंकि यह भी संशय था
कि संशय नहीं है
पर किसी को उम्मीद नहीं थी
कि संशय नहीं होगा

संशय तब नहीं होगा
लाल ने सफ़ेद से कहा
अदला-बदली कर लें

अपने-अपने रंग में उदास
बेरौनक़ हो रही है हमारी मौत

सफ़ेद तो किसी का निचोड़ नहीं
तुम सफ़ेद कैसे हो सकते हो
सफ़ेद ने कहा
जब कि मैं तो लाल हो लूंगा

लाल ने कहा
ऐसी हालत में जो भी हम दोनों हो सकते हों
एक होने के लिए वही हो जायें

चलो काले हो जाते हैं
सफेद ने कहा
बराबर-बराबर काले
फिर अपने रंग अलग-अलग नहीं मरेंगे

तब हम रंग से नहीं आश्चर्य से सफ़ेद
और क्रोध से लाल
दोनों की निन्दा में शब्द ढूंढ सकते हैं

Rebirth

there was grave uncertainty
that there was uncertainty
because there was even uncertainty
that uncertainty existed
no one had any hope
that it could be overcome

then it happened
and red said to white
you can change now

moody and sullen
our death stripped of its colors

white can't be anything's essence
how can you become white
white said
when I become red

red said
in our state of health
whatever we two can be
we should try to be the same

so you want to go black
white said
the same shade of black
then our colors won't clash

then we'll be white
not from color but from surprise
we'll be red from anger

तब तक साक्षात् काले ने कहा
तुम दोनों कितने ही काले क्यों न हो जाओ
लेकिन मेरे बराबर निचट्टू कोई नहीं होगा ।

renouncing both
we can find new words

then black reared his head and said
you two can turn as black as you want
you still won't be as black as me

बच्चे-१

चुपके से कोई गन्दगी रात और दिन
अपना स्मारक खड़ा कर रही है
और चुपके से
कुछ कम चीजोंवाली दुनिया को
कुछ ज़्यादा चीजोंवाली दुनिया में
ढकेल रही है

बच्चे
ज़िन्दगी के दरवाज़े पर हैं
जैसे कि ज़िन्दगी बच्चों का खेल हो
क्योंकि चुपके से
हमारी तोड़ी हुई
हमारी छोड़ी हुई चीज़ों को
वे सँवार रहे हैं

कूड़े के बग़ल में पैदा होकर
मामूली चीज़ों की महान खुशी में
जो अपने हाथ घायल कर रहे हैं
वे चुपके से हमारी नफ़रत में भी
कोई काम की चीज़ ढूँढ रहे हैं

ज्यों ही हम उनके कान पकड़ते हैं
वे हमारी कमज़ोरी पकड़ते हैं
चुपके से कोई उनको
वहाँ से नहीं पकड़ सकता
जहाँ से वे उग रहे होते हैं

इसलिए बच्चों को
चारों ओर से सींचो
पता नहीं वे कहाँ से उग रहे हैं

चींटी के साथ वे दीवार पर चढ़ रहे हैं
चुपके से

Children (I)

all day and night
trash is silently building its memorial
and silently
pushing a world of fewer things
into the world of more things

children
at the world's threshold
as though life were a child's game
because silently
they're arranging
our broken things
our discarded things

born next to the trash heap
in the great happiness of ordinary things
hurting their hands
silently searching
for some useful thing
through even our hatred

as soon as we grab them by the ear
they seize upon our weakness
silently
no one can remove them
from where they're growing

so sprinkle water all over
the kids
we don't know where they're growing

they're climbing the wall with the ants
silently

पोड़ों को जड़-सहित देख रहे हैं
और चिड़िया अगर बोल नहीं सकती
तो आखिर वह कह क्या रही है ?

वे फूल का एक-एक रेशा नोचते हैं
कि आखिर खुशबू कहाँ पर है
सारा फूल फेंककर
केवल खुशबू को वे पकड़ लेना चाहते हैं
वे स्टोव के अन्दर बैठकर
भरभरा रहे हैं
टोपियों में भौंरे पकड़कर
दम घुटने का गाना सुन रहे हैं

सारी तीलियों का बारूद जलाने के बाद
माचिस की डिब्बी को छेद-छेदकर
वे दरवाज़े और खिड़कियाँ बना रहे हैं
चारों ओर
अधजली तीलियाँ रोपकर
वे बैग लगा रहे हैं

नींद में डूबने के बाद
अपने-अपने घरों निकलकर
सपने में
वे इसमें खेलेंगे
और उससे ज़्यादा सीखेंगे
जागते में जितना नहीं सीख पाते

नदी में लेकर टंकी तक
टंकी से लेकर नल तक
वे छरछरा रहे हैं
घूमते हुए शहर को
वे किसी झील के अन्दर घूम रहे हैं

आज के इस चितकबरे दिन को
उजाले से भरे हुए समूचे दिन को
वे फूल पर बैठी

they're watching the trees
roots and all
and if the bird can't speak
then what's it saying?

they pluck out each stamen from the flower
looking for the sweet scent
throwing the whole flower away
they only want to keep the scent
they sit in the stove
burning up
catching black bees in hats
listening to the song of suffocation

after burning the sulfur off the matches
after breaking apart the matchbox
they're making a door and windows
and all around
sticking the half-burnt matchsticks
in the ground to make a garden

drowned in sleep
they leave their homes
to go play
in their dreams
where they will learn more
than during their waking hours

from the river to the water tank
from the tank to the irrigation pipe
they're burning up
they're wandering through the city
they're wandering inside a lake

in today's speckled world
like a butterfly

तितली की तरह देख रहे हैं

और उस तितली को
जिसमें हम सबके प्राण शामिल हैं
चुपके से
मुट्ठो में बन्द करना चाहते हैं

रात को वे कहीं से
गिरती हुई देखना चाहते हैं
अँधेरे को मसलकर
महसूस करना चाहते हैं

बड़ी-से-बड़ी जगह के
छोटे-से-छोटे अँधेरे में
घरों के कोनों में
चारपाइयों और मेज़ों के नीचे
एक जो निरर्थक अँधेरा होता है
हमारा 'हौव्वा'
उनका पीछा
वहाँ से शुरू करता है

वे आनेवाले वर्षों में
आनेवाले दिनों को पकड़ेंगे
जैसे कभी
अश्वमेध के घोड़े पकड़े जाते थे
चुनौती देते हुए
किसी भी समय
आकाश से
वे हमारे फेफड़ों में उतर रहे हैं
इसे साफ़ रखना ज़रूरी है ।

they're sitting on a flower
watching the world
all through the light-bright day

they want to capture
this butterfly in their fists
silently
this butterfly
that is a part of us all

they want to see
night mysteriously fall
they want to know what it feels like
to grind down the darkness

there
in some tiny darkness
inside some vast space
in the corners of homes
beneath beds and tables
this senseless darkness
like a chimera
starts to follow them

in the years to come
they will take hold of the days
as sometimes
the king's horse would be stolen
in an act of defiance
any moment now
from the sky
they'll enter into our lungs
that we must keep clean

मौलिकता

जड़ें
वही हों

उसी तने पर
वे ही टहनियाँ हों

ज्यादा अच्छे लगते हैं
तब
नये पत्ते

वरना नये पौधे में वे होते ही हैं ।

Origins

if those
are roots

if that trunk
has branches

it will be
prettier
with new leaves

harbored now
within
the sapling

आधार

उस औरत ने कुछ नहीं बताया
उस पुरुष से
घृणा का आधार

आज ;
एक हलकी-सी आहट है
अगली दुश्मनी छिपाये रखने की

ये था भविष्य

इधर आओ बच्चे !
मरे हुए दिनों का अनुभव
वो रहा तुम्हारा पिता ।

Our Future

that woman said nothing
to that man
to make him hate her

today
a little rest
hiding from tomorrow's
enemy

this is our future

come here my child!
your father
is what happened
in days gone by

एक बुढ़िया का इच्छागीत

जब मैं लगभग बच्ची थी
हवा कितनी अच्छी थी

घर से जब बाहर को आयी
लोहार ने मुझे दराँती दी
उससे मैंने घास काटी
गाय ने कहा दूध पी

दूध से मैंने, घी निकाला
उससे मैंने दिया जलाया
दीये पर एक पतंगा आया
उससे मैंने जलना सीखा

जलने में जो दर्द हुआ तो
उससे मेरे आँसू आये
आँसू का कुछ नहीं गढ़ाया
गहने की परवाह थी

घास-पात पर जुगनू चमके
मन में मेरे भट्टी थी
मैं जब घर के भीतर आयी
जुगनू-जुगनू लुभा रहा था
इतनी रात इकट्टी थी ।

जब मैं लगभग बच्ची थी

The Old Woman's Song of Herself as a Young Girl

when I was a young girl
the breeze was so fresh!

when I left the house
the blacksmith gave me a sickle
that I used to cut grass
for the cow
that told me to drink its milk

from milk I made butter
that I used to make an oil lamp
where a moth came
to teach me about fiery death

from the pain of burning
came my tears
which led to nothing
they died so soon

fireflies flickered in the fields
my mind was my forge
when I went inside
the fireflies enticed me back out
the night was so dark!

प्रेमप्रसंग

ज्यों ही उन पुरानी यादगारों से
एक बड़ा-सा पेपरवेट बनाना चाहता हूँ
त्यों ही वह बनकर
दूर एक स्निग्ध मेज पर चला जाता है

जहाँ मेरे और तुम्हारे हाथ
एक अविस्मरणीय मृदुता में
साँपो की तरह गुँथे पड़े हैं

(उन्हें इस भारी पेपरवेट से
दबाना नहीं चाहता)

फिर ज्यों ही
उन पुरानी यादगारों से
एक बहुत बड़ा हथियार बनाना चाहता हूँ
त्यों ही
वह बनकर आकाश में तन जाता है

जहाँ हमारी
पुराने उद्देश्यों में चमकती
—गरदनें हैं
जिनमें अगर आज भी
एक घूँट समय डाल दिया जाय
तो ख़ून
नसों में दौड़ता दिखायी देगा

(मगर चालू अँधेरे को
दो ऑंखें देने से पहले
उन्हें काटना नहीं चाहता)

फिर भी ज्यों ही उन पुरानी यादगारों से
ज़िन्दगी के बारे में
एक प्रस्ताव बनाना चाहता हूँ

Affairs of the Heart

from those old memories
I want to make a hefty paperweight
that immediately
departs for my beloved's distant table

where your hands and mine
are entwined in unforgettable softness
like snakes in their den

(I don't want to hold them down
with this heavy paperweight)

from those memories
I want to build a massive weapon
that rises into the sky to be pulled taut

where
there are glittering necks
in our old intentions
where
if a little time is added
even today
blood
will be seen coursing through their veins

(but I don't want to cut out my eyes
before giving them
to the cunning darkness)

from those memories
I want to write some guidelines for life
yet immediately
every single word renounces

त्यों ही सारे शब्द
वर्णमाला की मूल सदस्यता से
त्यागपत्र देकर
विरोध में उठ खड़े होते हैं

(लेकिन मैं पहले ही झटक में
उनका क्रोध
निलम्बित नहीं करना चाहता)

तब सोचता हूँ
उन पुरानी यादगारों के बीच
जो एक चिनगारी है
उसी से सबके इरादे प्रज्वलित करूँ

बस इतनी ही में
हरे वनखण्डों से
धुआँ उठने लगता है

(इतनी जल्दी हरियाली को
आग और आँसू के सुपुर्द करना
ठीक होगा ?)

सोचते-सोचते
अन्त में कुछ नहीं बना पाता हूँ
न वे पुराने हाथ
न चमकती हुई ऊष्ण गरदनें
न कोई झलझलाता हुआ प्रस्ताव
न कोई अग्निपुंज

हमारी कई चीज़ों को
ऐतिहासिक कीचड़ के साथ
बहा ले जाती
अथाह काली बाढ़
मेरी पीठ को
लगातार किनारा बनाकर काटती
अब कन्धे और सिर को डूबोना चाहती है

its place
in the alphabet
and raises its voice in opposition

(from the first blow
I don't want to minimize
their anger)

then I think
how in all those memories
there's an ember
I will stoke
to illuminate intentions

and just like that
smoke will rise
from the green forests

(will it be okay
to give the forests
to fire and tears
so quickly?)

nothing comes
from all my thinking
not those old hands
not glistening feverish necks
not a shimmering idea
not a pillar of fire

a bottomless black flood
takes away our things
wrapped in the mud of history
she laps insistently at my back
now she wants to drown
my shoulders and head

ऐसे मौके पर जो पैरों के नीचे है
इस ज़मीन को चाहता हूँ
कि थोड़ा और ऊपर उठा लूँ

ताकि शिकंजों में फँसी
हमारी गरदनें
हमारे सिर और कन्धे
अपनी उपस्थिति को
आनेवाले दिनों की रोशनी में
प्रसंगवश चमका सकें

और जो भी देखे अपनी यादगारों से
उसे न पेपरवेट बनाना पड़े
न कल्पित हथियार
वल्कि विरोध में उठे हुए शब्दों को
वह एक ऐसे वाक्य को दे दे
जो हरी घास पर
भरी बन्दूक की तरह रखा हुआ हो ।

at times like this
I wish I could raise
the ground beneath my feet
just so much

so that our shackled necks
heads and shoulders
could transform themselves
in the light of the days to come
and glisten and glimmer

and whatever is seen
through the eyes of memory
must not be made into paperweights
or imaginary weapons
but into words raised in protest
a voice
like a heavy gun
laid in the green grass

मेरी कथा

मेरी कथा
फावड़ा घिस जाने की
कारखाना उजड़ जाने की
सड़क टूट जाने की कथा है

मेरी कथा
पत्थर के रेत हो जाने की
पेड़ के
लकड़ी हो जाने की
कोयले के
आग ही जाने की कथा है

मेरी कथा
जाने हो जाने की कथा है ।

My Story

my story
is a story about
a worn spade
a shuttered factory
a rough road

my story
is a story about
rock turned to sand
trees turned to kindling
charcoal turned to fire

my story
is a story
of endless change

चिड़िया-२

वो चिड़िया जो अब नहीं है
ये चिड़िया उसके बच्चों में से एक है

जैसी कि यह है
इसको वैसा बनानेवाले पंखों के सिरे
बादलों की रगड़ से धुले हुए हैं

फेफड़ों में पृथ्वी के
गरम भपारे हैं
जो वर्षों से खायी जा रही है
इसकी उड़ान देखो
ये वो चिड़िया है
जिसकी चोंच में नए घोंसले के लिए
पुराने तिनके हैं

इसी की वजह से
आसपास के बीचोंबीच
हमारी नजर टिक रही है
अपने शरीर के छोटे-से द्वीप में

ये वो चिड़िया है
जिसे लोग खौलते हुए पानी में डालते हैं

ताकि इसके पोशाक बने हुए पंख
एक चिड़िया को चिड़िया बनानेवाले पंख
सब्ज़ी के छिलकों के साथ
रसोई के पीछे फेंके जा सकें

जहाँ ये अक्सर आती है
हमारे बच्चों के जूठन में से
अपने बच्चों का स्वादिष्ट भोजन लेने के लिए

The Bird (II)

this bird is one of the babies
of the bird that has died

each bird is made into a bird
when the tips of its new wings
are washed by rubbing against the clouds

in its lungs
is the earth's warm vapor
being exhaled for years
watch it fly!
this is the bird
carrying old twigs in its beak
to its nest

and
we stare into the midst of the sky
its body is a tiny island
this is the bird
that people throw into boiling water

because its wings are its clothes
its wings
that are given from bird to bird
can be thrown out behind the kitchen
with the vegetable peels

where one often returns
to take the leftovers from our children's plates
that become its children's tastiest treats

इसके पेट की धारियों में
किसी के बच्चे की स्वेटर का
कितना अच्छा डिज़ाइन है

ये वो चिड़िया है
जिसे रात की एक-एक पसली का पता है
जो आकाश की
एक-एक कोर का रंग जानती है
और
जिसकी आँख का हर कोया लाल है

ये वो चिड़िया है जिसका जूड़ा
शहर की
किसी भी सुन्दर लड़की के जूड़े से
ज़्यादा असली है

ये वो चिड़िया है जिसकी एक आँख में
पतझर के आखिरी पत्ते का पतन
और दूसरी आँख में
वसन्त के उतावले प्रसव की सूचना है

ये वो चिड़िया है जिसकी छाती
अपने बच्चों के लिए
किसी भी स्तनोंवाली छाती से
ज़्यादा ज़रूरी है

जब हरेक पत्ती के नीचे से
धुआँ निकल रहा हो
झीलें तक गुम हो गयी हों
जंगल
दमकलों की तरह सीटियाँ मार रहा हो
मौसम अपने जूते तक न बचा पा रहा हो

तब अपनी ही उड़ान से थकी
कंघी-जैसी छाती से बिखरती
इस चिड़िया की आवाज़

the stripes on its breast
make a wonderful pattern
for a child's sweater

this is the bird
that knows the night's every rib
that knows the color
of the sky's every nook
and
whose eyes plumb the depths of red

this is the bird
whose twin is more real
than the twin
of a beautiful girl in the city

this is the bird
in whose one eye
there is the last leaf of fall
and in whose other eye
there is the news
of the spring baby's hasty birth

this is the bird
whose breast is more important
than the breasts
where babies nurse

when smoke has spread
from beneath every leaf
when the bird has flown
above the lakes
when the forest
whistles its fire alarm
when the day and the night
the clouds and the air

आग लगने के बाद
जंगल में
आग लगने से पहले का जंगल खोज रही है

याददाश्त के ठिकानों पर
जंगली जानवरों के रोंगटे खड़े हैं
कोई चीज़ पहली बार
किसी चीज़ के विरोध से मिल रही यही

इसलिए जब कहता हूँ कि 'जे वो चिड़िया है'
आग में जो इस बार जिन्दा जलेगी
तब इस सवाल का कोई मतलब नहीं रह जाता
कि आखिर इस जवान चिड़िया का नाम क्या है ?

क्योंकि वक्त मेरे सामने एक दूसरा सवाल है
(खामोशी जिसका पहला जवाब है)
कि अगर ये वो चिड़िया है
तो फिर डर किस चिड़िया का नाम है ?

are brought to their knees

tired of flying
the bird's voice spreads
from its frayed breast feathers
after the fire
looking in the forest for the forest
before the fire

in the folds of memory
the hair on the backs of the wild animals
stands on end
for the first time
something met with resistance

so when I say this is the bird
that now will burn alive in the fire
the problem of this baby bird's name
is meaningless

because now there is a more meaningful question
(whose answer is only silence)
if this is that bird
then which bird is named fear?

यहाँ से शुरू हुए

यहाँ से शुरू हुए
कि बिना कुछ पाये
आनन्द क्यों नहीं ?

आँख खुली तो चौंके
कि जो दिखा नहीं
क्या था ?

डरानेवाले को
डराना चाहते थे
निडर होने के लिए
यहाँ से शुरू हुए

बारह हज़ार वर्ष पहले
और बाद भी
जो पहले ही निडर हैं
वे किस डर से पैदा हुए ?

अगर इतना ही जानते
कि नहीं जानते
तो भी कोई बात नहीं थी

दुख यहाँ से शुरू हुए
कि जानना चाहते हैं
रात में
रात के अलावा जो कुछ है
दिन में
दिन के अलावा भी
जानना चाहते हैं

Things Begin Here

—things begin here
and so without finding anything
why couldn't there be happiness?

my eyes opened
I shook with surprise
what was there
inside what couldn't be seen?

some wanted
to scare those who scare others
in order to remain fearless
—things begin here

twelve thousand years ago
and twelve thousand years from now
those who are born fearless
are born from what fear?

if all they know
is that they don't know
it wouldn't matter

sadness begins here
wanting to know
what there is in the night
other than the night
wanting to know
what there is in the day
other than the day

वर्तमान में भूत
किसी भी समय
दबोच सकता है
इस बात से
कि बच्चे कहीं डर न जायें
बड़े डर रहे हैं ।

today ghosts
can seize us
at any moment
because
we worry
about protecting our children
from fear

मुझे उगाओ

मेरे चुम्बनअगर वृक्ष भी होंगे
तो भी तुम उन्हें
अपने होठों पर उगा लोगी
ओ मेरे आकाश में
घूमती हुई पृथ्वी !

मैं ही हूँ
वह एक नयी व्यवस्था
जिसे अब भी वसन्त कहते हैं
और जिसके लिए वनस्पतियाँ
बार-बार यशस्वी होती हैं

ओ मेरी पृथ्वी !
वक्षज पर्वतों के मुख
तुमने
विषैली हवाओं में विकसित
आकाश के नीले होंठों पर
टिका दिये हैं
तुम निरर्थक ही उदार नहीं हो

तुम्हारी उदारता
और मेरे चुम्बन
ज़िन्दगी के इलाके में
जंगल हो सकते हैं
जिसमें
हजारों चिड़ियों की गरमाहट होगी

तुम मेरी नज़र में घूम रही हो
और मैं तुम्हारी खिड़की से
पड़ती रोशनी में
आलपिन की तरह चमक रहा हूँ

Raise Me Up!

my agarwood trees
will be there too
and you will raise them
from your lips
O my earth spinning
in the heavens!

here it's just me
and this is new to us
what we still call spring
and love
for its verdant life

O my earth!
you have placed
the faces of the voluptuous mountains
on the blue lips of the sky
in poisonous winds
your generosity isn't meaningless

your generosity
and my agarwood trees
can be forests
in life's remote lands
where
the warmth of thousands of birds
will be found

I watch you spin
and in the resplendent light
outside your window
I'm glistening like a sewing pin

मुझे उन बीती रातों
बीते दिनों में चुभो दो
ख़ून अब ज़मीन पर फैलना चाहता है

मेरे चुम्बन अगर युद्ध भी हैं
तो तुम उन्हें लड़ोगी
तब मैं योद्धाओं की आत्मा
और शहीदों का बलिदान लेकर
तुम्हारे होंठों पर चमक उठूँगा

मेरी भाषा
पंख फड़फड़ायेगी
जब अन्याचार होगा
मेरी भाषा पंख फड़फड़ायेगी
तब अगर तुम
थोड़ा भी फुसफुसा सको
मैं समझूँगा
तुमने मुझे धारण कर लिया है

मुझे धारण करना
जिस तरह तुम अपनी बाहें
दस ओर फैलाकर
आकाश को धारण करती हो

ओ मेरी पृथ्वी
ओ मेरी घूमती हुई पृथ्वी
मैं जूझना चाहता हूँ
मुझे उगाओ !

thrust me into
the days and nights of the past
now that blood wants to spread across the earth

if my kisses are war
you will fight them off
I will take on the soul of soldiers
and the sacrifice of martyrs
and glisten on your lips

when tortured
my words
will flap their wings
my words will flap their wings
if you can whisper to me
even just a little
I'll understand
that you've encompassed me

you encompass me
as you spread
your arms in ten directions
and encompass the sky

O my earth!
O my spinning earth!
I want to taste strife!
raise me up!

कमरा और आदमी

केवल एक दिन पुरानी चीज़
इसकी नींव है
इससे एक दिन हमेशा पुरानी

मगर कुछ कम पुरानी चीज़ें
इस कमरे में
इस कमरे को सोने नहीं देंगी

नींव पर
मजबूत
बैठा हुआ कमरा
आत्मा में जिसकी
सामान ठुँसा है
आदमी की दाढ़ी को
सफेद होते देख रहा है

गूँगे मुँह में जो कभी
शब्द की तरह कभी सुपारी की तरह
एक-एक चीज़ के सिर को
चबाना चाहता है
पर कोई याद आया स्वाद
जीभ को बंजर बना देता है
एक दिन
इस सादे आकाश में
बनते कमरे को
धन्यवाद मिले थे

उनकी दुरुस्ती के लिए कारीगर
कहीं दूर
आज भी इसकी पीठ ठोक रहे हैं

अपनी काम पुरानी चीज़ों के साथ
इसमें फँसे

A Room, a Man

for anything that is just one day old
its foundation
is always one day older

but in this room
there are things that are slightly younger
that don't let this room sleep

a well-built room
laid on a foundation
with a soul
stuffed with possessions
watches the man's beard
turning white

a mute mouth
that wants to gnaw on things
gently
like words sometimes
like supari sometimes
but then a memory returns
a delicious taste
that keeps the tongue wanting
one day
in this empty sky
the growing room
received its thanks

to make it sturdy
today somewhere far away
workers are hammering at its back

आदमी के वास्ते
और कुछ पुरानी नींद लाओ

पाने के लिए
पुराने आकार का वह सपना गढ़ो
एक बार भी जो सच न हुआ हो

जूतों में से
पैर निकालने के लिए
ज्यों ही आदमी
कोने में जाता है
वर्षों से झुका हुआ
पूर्वज
कमरे का कैदी आकाश
उसका सिर सूँघता है

(सिर
जो बाज़ार में
पिछले पाँच साल से
बिना कीमत के घूमता रहा)

विचलित
कमरे में
हताश आदमी
बीस वर्ष दूर उठनेवाले बादल से
अनभिज्ञ है

इस बात से भी अनभिज्ञ
कि स्वाभाविक होने के लिए
इतना पुराना होना है
इतना पुराना कि कमरे की आँखों में
ये नयी चीज़ें
नींद की तरह आयी हुई
दिखायी दे सकें

for the man trapped inside
your things that are slightly younger
please bring a deeper sleep

and for water
build the dream of the old form
that was never real

whenever the man goes
into the corner
to remove his shoes
he catches the scent
of the old room's imprisoned air

(a man
who for the last five years
has wandered pointlessly
through the marketplace)

in the misplaced room
the desperate man
is unaware of
the clouds that will billow up
twenty years from now

he doesn't understand
why you have to be so old
to be natural
so old that
these new things
that come on like sleep
can be seen by the room

अपनी उम्र के
(जिसे कोई नहीं जानता)
उस बचे-खुचे हिस्से को
कमरे के हवाले करते हुए
आदमी सोचता है

कोई चीज़ नयी नहीं होती
बल्कि हर नयी चीज़
कुछ कम पुराने चीज़ होती है ।

the man thinks of
his remaining years
given over to the room
(no one knows his age)

there's nothing new
each new thing is only
something slightly less old

मैं अकेला नहीं हूँ

क्या कोई छेद खिड़की नहीं हो सकता
कि उजाला भीतर आ सके ?

क्या कोई छेद दरवाज़ा नहीं हो सकता
कि अँधेरा बाहर जा सके ?

अब मैं अकेला नहीं हूँ
तुम्हारे अन्धे प्रहार के इन्तज़ार में
— विस्फोट के लिए जो ज़रूरी है ।

I'm Not Alone

can a hole be a window
through which light can come?

can a hole be a door
through which the darkness can pass?

now I'm not alone
waiting for your blind assault
—and then the explosion

उजाला

सबके हाथों से गिरकर
उजाला
मिट्टी में मिल गया

वह वहीं से उगेगा
और हम अचानक देखने लगेंगे

देखने लगेंगे एक-दूसरे की थकान
थरथराती आँखें
पथराये चेहरे
मरे हुए लोगों की एक अच्छी-खासी दुनिया
हम देखने लगेंगे और उठ खड़े होंगे

हम चाहें और वह उगेगा
इस अग्निकाण्ड के बाद
हम फिर अपने तनों से
आकाश में घुस रहे होंगे

हवा में लहरा रहे होंगे हमारे उद्योगपत्र ।

Light

the light that falls
from everyone's hands
mixes with the earth

it will grow there
and suddenly we will begin to see

see each other's fatigue
drooping eyelids
stony faces
see the whole big world of the dead
and we'll get up

if we want
the light will grow
after this conflagration
and through our bodies
we will start to mix
with the sky

our words rippling in the wind

चिड़िया का प्रसव

माँ उस पुरानी घटना का नाम है

अपने पेट में अण्डे लेकर
चिड़िया बाज़ार में गयी

लाला के आगे से सुतली
घोड़े के आगे से घास
बूचड़ के आगे से बकरी के बाल
बच्चे के आगे से काग़ज़ लाकर
उसने घोंसला बनाया
जिसका विरोध नहीं किया जा सकता

प्रसव से पहले चिड़िया ने
घोंसला बना लिया था
चिड़िया का विरोध
आज़ादी का विरोध है

उस दरवाज़े से बाहर
उस आकाश में

जो आईने के अन्दर फँसा हुआ है
नयी चिड़िया
उस चिड़िया के साथ रहना चाहती है
आईने के भीतर से
जो चोंच लड़ाती है

आईना धोखा है
या चिड़िया खुद को नहीं पहचानती
मगर जितनी जिस रंग की आ जायें
उतनी उस रंग की
वो दिखा देता है

The Bird's Birth

ma
is the name of that lost moment

with eggs in her womb
the bird went to the market

from the shopkeeper she took twine
from the horse she took grass
from the butcher she took goat hair
from the child she took paper
and made a nest
and no one could stop her

before giving birth
the bird had made a nest
to hurt her
is to hurt freedom

outside that door
in that sky
trapped inside the mirror
the new bird
wants to be with the bird
that pecks at it
from inside the mirror

the mirror plays tricks
or the bird can't recognize itself
but however many birds
of however many colors come
the mirror reflects these birds
just as they are

चिड़िया अगर उस परत को
कमज़ोर बनाना चाहती है
जिसके पार
दूसरी चिड़िया फँसी है

तो भी उसका विरोध नहीं किया जा सकता
क्योंकि आईना भी एक दीवार है
चोंच चाहे बड़ी हो चाहे छोटी
भूख का ज़लज़ला एक है

चींटी जिसे ले गयी
हाथी
वो कण नहीं उठा सका

पानी जितना चिड़िया ने पिया
नदी कभी समुद्र तक नहीं पहुँचा सकी

एक चिड़िया की भूख
एक चींटी की भूख
एक हाथी की भूख ;
भूख चाहे किसी की हो
— मार एक है

शान्ति में, खामोशी में
सन्नाटे में
तसल्ली के बाद जो पैदा होती है
माँ उस इच्छा का नाम है ।

if the bird wants to weaken
the pane
inside which
the other bird is trapped

even then
no one can stop her
because the mirror too is a wall
whether the beak is large or small
hunger's earthquake is the same

the tiny thing that the ant picked up
the elephant
couldn't lift

the river couldn't bring to the sea
the water the bird drinks

one bird's hunger
one ant's hunger
one elephant's hunger—
whosoever's hunger it may be
—it feels the same

in peace in silence
in stillness
the desire that is born after comfort
its name is *ma*

सहयात्री

चाहे पेड़ भूल जायें
कि उन्हें पेड़ होना है
पत्ते अकड़ जायें
और जगह खाली न करें

लेकिन मेरे और अपने बारे में
जो कुछ तुम सोचती हो
वह कहीं भी
दुनिया के बारे में सोचने से
बाहर नहीं है

क्योंकि तुम
समूची मुझे याद हो
उस दुनिया में भी
जहाँ शब्द काम नहीं आते
मैं तुम्हें बोल सकता हूँ

यादों के जहाज़ का
वज़न उठाने के लिए
मेरे शरीर में
जितना ख़ून है
उसे लेकर
अब मैं एक पूरा समुद्र हूँ

चलते हुए जहाज़ के नीचे
दो हिस्सों में बँटा हुआ
तुम्हारे साथ — यात्री
और अपने साथ
— केवल समुद्र ।

Traveling Together

even if trees should forget
they have to be trees
even if leaves should fall
and not give themselves over to emptiness

still whatever you think
about me and you
will never exceed
what can be thought
about the world

because even if I remember you
just as you were
even in that world
where words are useless
I can still speak to you

to lift the weight of
the ship of memories
I took up all the blood
in my body
and became the open ocean

under the passing ship
two parts were formed
with you—the travelers
and with me
—the ocean

किसी ने मुझे देखा

आज किसी ने मुझे देखा
जैसे
कभी किसी को देखा ही न हो

वह भीतर तक
हाथ डालनेवाली नज़र थी

माँ ने देखा
कि एक और ने देखा
जो माँ भी हो सकती है
किसी दूसरे दरवाज़े से
मुझे
संसार दे दरवाज़े पर

भूख, ज़रूरत और अमरता
इनमें से
कौन-सी संस्कृति है माँ ?
मैं फिर से कायम होना चाहता हूँ
माँ
मेरे किस-किस रिश्ते की माँ है ?

क्या माँ केवल गर्भाशय है
तीस साल पीछे छूटा हुआ गर्भाशय ?
क्या वह केवल रोटी, कपड़ा और मकान है ?

नहीं ;
माँ तीस साल पहले
पिता के चुम्बनों को धारण करती
पुरुषों की असमर्थता को
हद की तरह फाँदती
एक स्त्री भी है ।

Someone Looked at Me

today someone looked at me
in a way
they had never looked at anyone before

it was like having
a hand reach inside me

mom saw
that someone else saw me
she who could be a mom to me
from another door
there I was
standing at the world's door

hunger need and immortality
where's the culture
in these, mom?
I want everything to be okay again
mom
in which ways is she mom?

is mom only a womb?
a womb thirty years ago?
is she only bread clothes and shelter?

no
thirty years ago
mom
accepted dad's kisses
leapt beyond men's weaknesses
—she's a woman too

कभी पति के हिस्से की
कभी मेरे-जैसे हिस्से की
जिसे औलाद कहते हैं
कभी जंगल-भर की

कभी सन्नाटे की
पर अपने हिस्से में
केवल उतनी
दूसरे जितना उसके हिस्से में हों
वह उड़ती फिरती
अगर कोई उसके पक्ष में होता
वह एक सपना भी थी
केवल दूध पिलानेवाला स्तन नहीं
न केवल अगली खुराक
न केवल फसलोंवाली ऋतु

माँ की मिट्टी
केवल एक ट्यूब नहीं
न केवल तापमान
न केवल
'एक सफल जन्मदात्री संस्था'
न जच्चा-बच्चा-केंद्र का कमरा

माँ उस चीख का नाम है
जो आँसुओं के कीचड़ को
ज़मीन की तरह सख्त बना देती है

आज किसी ने मुझे देखा
जैसे कि मुझको साफ़-साफ़ सुना हो ।

at times it was
that she leapt beyond my father's limitations
or those of people like me
—her offspring
then sometimes the whole forest's

or those of silence
but as for her own
they were no more than
what others had
—she helped people
and if anyone fell under her care
it was like a dream
not just breastfeeding
not just the next meal
or the harvest season

mom's earth
was not just a tube well
not just heat or cold
not just
"a successful birthing hospital"
not a room in the children's ward

mom is the name for that scream
that makes the mud's tears hard
like the earth's crust

today someone saw me
it was like they heard what I had to say

बच्चे-२

जिस कमरे में भी बच्चे सोये हुए हैं
बच्चे इस समय
उस कमरे में नहीं हैं

बच्चे सोये हुए हैं
मगर अपराध कर रहे हैं

इस वक्त उनकी नींद में
जानवर उतर रहे हैं
बच्चे इस समय उस कमरे में नहीं है

अगर हैं
तो वहाँ कई चीज़ों टूट-फूट रही हैं
मुझे वहाँ पहुँच जाना चाहिए
जहाँ उनके दोस्त
उनके लिए खतरा पैदा कर रहे हैं

जिस कमरे में भी बच्चे सोये हुए हैं
वहाँ घोड़े बच्चों को कुचल रहे हैं

बाघ
बच्चों को उठाना चाहते हैं
साँप
बच्चों का पीछा कर रहे हैं

बच्चे सोये हुए हैं
मगर हाँफ रहे हैं

मैं उनकी नींद में घुसना चाहता हूँ
वे क्यों चिल्ला रहे हैं ?
उन्हें बिना जगाये
मैं उनके सपने में जाना चाहता हूँ
जिससे देख सकूँ

Children (II)

even in the room
where kids are sleeping
there are no kids

the kids are asleep
but up to no good

their dreams are filled
with animals
but now there are no kids
in that room

if there were kids there
then all sorts of things would be breaking
I should go
where their friends
make life dangerous for them

even in the room where the kids are asleep
there are horses trampling them
lions and tigers
want to kidnap them
snakes
follow them

the kids are asleep
but they're huffing and puffing

I want to enter their dreams
(why are they screaming?)
without waking them
I want to enter their dreams
to see

कि उन्हें
डण्डा लेकर पीट तो नहीं रहा हूँ ?

if it's me who's beating them
with the schoolmaster's stick

कल के लिए

नींद से ढकी दुनिया में
धंसती हुई गोली की आवाज़ सुनकर
फूलदान में पानी डाल रही है लड़की

नींद से ढकी हुई दुनिया में
मोजे उतारकर
नंगे पैरों की चमक देखकर
छाती के बटन
ठीक से लगा रही है लड़की

नींद से ढकी हुई दुनिया में
खिड़की से बना
एक पुल
नदी से मिले हुए जंगल में
उतरता है
जिसे कल के लिए
पत्तों से ढककर छिपा रही है लड़की ।

For Tomorrow

deep in some sleepy world
having heard the sound of a muffled bullet
the girl is filling the vase with water

deep in some sleepy world
having taken off her socks
to see how her bare feet shine
the girl is sewing a button to her shirt

deep in some sleepy world
in the forest that meets the river
a bridge
made out of windows
descends
and the girl covers it with leaves
to save
for tomorrow

चलती रेल में

अगली शताब्दी के अन्तिम चरण में
हमने कहाँ पर की होंगी ये बातें
चलती रेल में
कहाँ पर की होंगी ?

मैंने कहा
दुनिया अगर एक उखड़ा हुआ
दरख्त होती
और में आरा होता
तो मेरे हिस्से क्या आता ?
सिवाय घिसायी के
सिवाय शरीर को दांत बना देने के
मेरे हिस्से क्या आया होता ?

उसने कहा
तुम अगर आरा होते
मैं अगर रेती होती
तो बताओ मेरे हिस्से क्या आया होता ?
किस काम आती अपनी रेताई

किस काम आता तुम्हारा दाँत होना
और किस काम आता
भीतर की सन्धि का
बेवजह बुरादा ?
रेतती मैं तुमको
तुम किसी और को रेतते
जैसा भी सोच लूँ कोई उपयोग नहीं

हमने कहाँ पर की होंगी ये बातें
चलती रेल में
कहाँ पर की होंगी ?
बाहर किस तारीख का अँधेरा रहा होगा ?

In the Passing Train

in the last moments of the next century
where will we speak about these things
in the passing train
where will we have spoken?

I said
if the world was an uprooted tree
and I were a saw
what would be left for me?
apart from what is worn out
apart from turning my body into teeth
what would be left for me?

and it said
if you were a saw
and I were a file
tell me what would be left for me?
what would be the point of my filing?
what would be the point of your teeth?
and what would be the point of
all the sawdust not yet shed
inside the tree?
if I file you down
you file someone else down
think about it
there's no point to it

where will we have spoken about these things
in the passing train
where will we have spoken?
and outside in the darkness what will the date be?

मैंने कहा
खुद हम अपने चेहरे नहीं चूम सकते
हमें एक-दूसरे की ज़रूरत है
जिनको भूख नहीं
उनके पेट नहीं होगा
हमारे पास तो दोनों हैं
अब अपने को जैसा भी सोच लें ?

चेहरे के गहन रंगों में
बातों के जहाज़ तैराती
वह बोली
अपने आलस्य में हम बिल्कुल अकेले हैं
और अपनी फूर्ति में
चाहे मैं आग होती
और मान लो कि अपनी आड़ में

दुनिया कम भयानक जंगल होती
(याने कि आग जिसकी
ऊपर दिखायी दे सकती)
सबकुछ जब राख हो जाता
तो मेरे हिस्से क्या आता ?
क्या आता एक श्मशान के अलावा
जिसमें मैं नहीं होती
मैं जो न धुआँ थी न कोयला न रख
मैं जो आग थी

रात में सफर था
सफर में रात थी
हमारा सफर था कि रात का सफर था ?

मैं जो बहुत दूर
किसी द्वीप से लौट रहा था
उसके चेहरे पर तैरते जहाज़ में
मैंने कहा
अगर हम लोहा होते
कील-कब्ज़ों में बंटा हुआ लोहा,

I said
we can't kiss our own faces
we need each other
those who aren't hungry
must not have stomachs
we have both
now what should we make of ourselves?

in the face's deep contours
our conversation pushed along like a ship
she said
we're completely alone
in our languor and our passion
if I were fire
(a fire that can be
seen from above)
and let's say the world in its span
becomes a tame wilderness
when everything is turned to ashes
then what will be left for me?
what will there be except a funeral pyre
where I will not be found?
I who am neither smoke nor coals nor ashes
I who was fire

the journey was at night
during the journey night fell
was it our journey or the night's journey?

I was coming back
from a distant island
aboard the passing ship of her face
I said
if we were steel
(steel turned into nails and screws)
if there was wood

लकड़ी होते
चौखट-दरवाज़े में बँटी हुई लकड़ी,
नाव की पेंदी के जोड़ होते
तो कहीं-न-कहीं
एक मज़बूती के लिए चस्पाँ रहते

वह बोली
पर तब भी क्या हम अपने बारे में
कुछ नहीं सोचते ?
जो कुछ हम हैं
पहचानने को
— बाकी हैं

इससे ज़्यादा इन्तज़ार
इससे ज़्यादा अपरिचय
हमारे हिस्से क्या आता ?

अपना सामान बदलते हुए
हमने कहाँ पर की होंगी ये बातें
चलती हुई रेल में
कहाँ पर की होंगी
अगली शताब्दी के अन्तिम चरण में ?

(wood turned into a doorframe)
if there was the seam of the boat's hull
then somewhere
there would be a seal ensuring strength

she said
but still do we ever think
about ourselves?
what we are
still escapes us

more waiting is needed
more knowledge
what will be left for us?

changing our bags
where will we speak about these things
in the passing train
where will we have spoken
in the last moments of the next century?

एकान्त के जबड़े पर

एकान्त के जबड़े पर मेरा प्यार
समूची पृथ्वी के बराबर है
सौ दिनों के बराबर रोशनी से चमकता

ऐसी आवाज़ों से भरा
जैसी शब्दों की घाटी में
नहीं गूँजती

बल्कि कुछ वैसी
जैसी आवाज़ें
बैल के कन्धे में गूँजती हैं
और उसे ऊपर उठा देती हैं
जहाँ से मरने के बाद भी
वे नहीं निकल पातीं

जैसी टीले के भीतर
चींटियों के सफर में
जैसी साँप के सरकने में
कुछ वैसी आवाज़ें
जैसी खरगोश के बड़े होते
कान के आकार में होती हैं

आज का दिन
सारी पृथ्वी के बराबर है
और सारी पृथ्वी
एकान्त के जबड़े पर
मेरे प्यार के बराबर है
जो हर उसके बराबर है
जिसकी गूँज
शब्दों में पहले से नहीं है ।

In the Jaws of Seclusion

in the jaws of seclusion
my love is as large as the whole world
glistening in the light of a hundred days

filled with voices
like those
that in the valley of words
don't resound

but are like
those echoing in the shoulder of an ox
to raise it up
from where the sounds cannot emerge
even after dying

like in the ant's journey
inside the anthill
or in the snake's winding path
there are sounds
like the sounds
in the outline
of the rabbit's large ears

today
is as big as the whole earth
and the whole earth
is as big as my love
in the jaws of seclusion
my love
which is as big as
everything whose echo
was never a part of language

चालाकी की शुरुआत

डेढ़ छैल के मुल्क में
दो छैल आये हैं
बहुतों को ठगेंगे
ठगायी नहीं देंगे

घोड़ा लटकाये, पान बाँधे, कटार खाये
बबलू ने पप्पू से कहा
'जो देख रहे हो मुझे भी दिखाओ'

'कुछ नहीं ; कहीं कुछ नहीं
कुछ भी तो नहीं मैं देख रहा हूँ' — पप्पू ने कहा

बबलू नहीं माना कि वह कुछ कैसे है
जो नहीं दिख रहा
ज़रूर कुछ है
जिसे तुम देख रहे हो

एक जगह
एक ही कोने पर खड़े
दोनों एक ही दिशा में देखते रहे
कि ज़रूर कुछ है

'तुम क्या समझे
मैं क्या देख रहा हूँ?'
और कहीं और देखा किया पप्पू
जहाँ से वह बड़ों-जैसा होकर आ रहा था

बिना आँख झपकाये
मोहित चेहरे पर अनुभव फैलाये
बबलू बोला
'समझ रहा हूँ तुम बिल्ली देख रहे हो
चिड़िया देख रहे हो
किले के भीतर जो बगीचा है

The Tale of Two Clever Boys

in the kingdom of cleverness
there were two clever little boys
ready to trick the world
and never be tricked themselves

they clambered down the road
like real thugs at a trot
chewing paan and brandishing daggers

Babaloo said to Pappu,
"tell me what you're looking at"

"it's nothing, it's nothing,
I'm not looking at anything," Pappu said

Babaloo shot back,
        "no, what is it?
you're looking at something
for sure"

standing in the same place
at the exact same bend in the road
looking in the exact same direction
there had to be something

"what did you think
I was looking at?" Pappu said
making like he was looking somewhere else
like an adult would do to fool someone

without blinking
Babaloo looked at his beloved Pappu's
face and surmised

उसमें घुसकर
एक फूल देख रहे हो'

अपनी छोटी-सी निकर में पप्पू
बबलू के साथ
बड़ों-जैसा बोला
'तुम ठीक समझ रहे हो
वहाँ बिल्ली चिड़िया को देख रही है
और चिड़िया एक भुनगे को
और उनके बीच एक फूल
राजकुमार का सर है
तोड़ दूँ ?
फटक पर सन्तरी का सर है
जैसे ठूँठ पर कौवा
उड़ाओगे ?'

बबलू ने पप्पू को बिना छुए पकड़ा
'समझता था
कि जो देख रहे हो
छिपा रहे हो
मैं तुम्हें देख रहा था
कि तुम क्या देख रहे हो ?
कुछ मैं भी देखूँगा
तो बिल्कुल नहीं दिखाऊँगा'

पप्पू ने बबलू को
एक दृश्य की तरह चाँपा

बबलू बोला
'कल मैंने एक साँप देखा
जिसके मुँह में लड़की थी
वह मैंने छीन ली
साँप बिचारा मर गया
पर मैं जानता हूँ कहाँ उसके अण्डे हैं
न लड़की बताऊँगा न साँप
न तुम्हें उसके अण्डे बताऊँगा'

"I'm thinking you're looking
at a cat or at a bird
or you've entered
the garden inside the castle
and you're looking at a flower"

in his tight little shorts
Pappu spoke to Babaloo
with adult-like assurance
"oh, you've got it right
a cat is looking at a bird
and the bird is looking at a wasp
and between them there's a flower
a prince's head
should I rip it off?
there's a sentry's head on the gate
like a crow on a stump
will you make it fly away?"

without having understood a thing
Babaloo answered
"I thought
that you were hiding from me
whatever you were looking at
I was looking at you
wondering what you were looking at
because if I'd seen something
I wasn't going to tell you"

Pappu looked at Babaloo
like he was speaking from far away

Babaloo spoke
"I saw a snake yesterday
with a stick in its mouth
I snatched it out

पप्पू फिर सारे दृश्य से बाहर ले गया
अपने हाथ
अपनी आँखें
अपना दिमाग
और खड़ा रहा
बबलू को बिना दौड़े, बिना छुए
घेरता हुआ बोला
— 'मैंने कल एक घोंसला देखा
उसमें चिड़िया के अण्डे हैं
अगले हफ्ते वह बच्चे निकालेगी
वे बच्चे मेरे हैं'

बबलू बोला
'मैं तुम्हें साँप के अण्डे बताऊँगा
तुम मुझे चिड़िया के अण्डे बताओ'

पप्पू ने झटके से दे मारा — 'क्यों ?'

बबलू ने पप्पू को
ऐसे फुसलाया
जैसे ये पकड़ में
अब आया तब आया
— साँप के अण्डे
हम घोंसले में रख देंगे
चिड़िया दोनों से बच्चे निकालेगी
तब तुम्हारे पास भी साँप होंगे
और मेरे पास भी चिड़िया होगी
सोच लो ?

'तिलचब्बन'
'गोबरपत्थन'
दो बूढ़े उनके पास से गुजरे
बतियाते
— सड़क — सड़क ये सड़क —
कितनी अच्छी जा रही है

the poor snake died
I know where its eggs are
but I won't tell where they are
the stick the snake or its eggs"

Pappu took possession of
his own hands
eyes and mind
and stood there
thinking he could do better than Babaloo
"I saw a nest yesterday
with eggs in it
next week they'll hatch
and the hatchlings will be mine"

Babaloo answered
"if I tell you where the snake eggs are
will you tell me where the bird eggs are?"

Pappu replied sharply
"why?"

Babaloo came up
with something
right then and there
to tempt Pappu
"we'll put the snake eggs in the nest
the mommy bird will raise the birds
and the snakes
then you'll have snakes
and I'll have birds
what do you think?"

then two old men
Tilchabban and Gobarpathan
crossed paths with them

— ऋतु बदल रही है तिलचब्बन,
एक-एक रोड़े पर मस्ती आ रही है
— अरे गोबरपत्थन ! ये बच्चे
ही-ही-ही बेचारे बच्चे
— बेफिक्कर बेचारे बच्चे
— असल उम्मर तो ये है पत्थन
— न कोई मतलब बज्र पड़े से
न कोई मतलब आग लगे से

पप्पू ने बबलू को, बबलू ने पप्पू को
तिलचब्बन, गोबरपत्थनवाले लहजे में
पूछा
— सड़क — सड़क ये हमारी
घरवाली सड़क है न ?
— हाँ, ये घरवाली
सड़क है

इसके बाद वे दोनों अलग हो गए
दोनों ख़ामोश
दोनों परेशान
पर दोनों जैसे किसी खदान में झाँक रहे हों

पप्पू जब घर लौटा
तो माँ की परेशानियों का अन्त नहीं था
चारों ओर पप्पू सवाल-ही-सवाल
और ऊपर से धौंस
कि तुमको कल बताऊँगा
मैंने आज क्या-क्या देखा
पर तू मुझे एक घोंसला ढूँढ दे
नहीं तो बबलू न मुझे कुछ देगा
न कुछ दिखायेगा

chatting away
"this street's not bad, you know"
"the weather's turning, Tilchabban,
it's getting more and more delightful
with every step"
"hey, Gobarpathan, look at these kids,"
he couldn't stop laughing, "poor kids!"
"what poor silly little kids!"
"being a kid is the best, Gobarpathan!"
"they don't know up from down!"

then Pappu turned to Babaloo
and Babaloo turned to Pappu
and asked each other
like they were
Tilchabban and Gobarpathan
talking to each other
"this road is the one
that leads home right?"
"yeah, it's the road home"

then the two of them parted ways
both silent
both upset
and both staring blankly ahead as if into the void

when Pappu got home
he hounded his mom
with endless questions
"I'll tell you tomorrow
what I saw today
but first find me a nest
or else Babaloo won't give me anything
and won't show me what he's found"

बबलू जब घर पहुँचा
तो उसकी माँ की परेशानियों का अन्त नहीं था
चारों ओर बबलू के सवाल-ही-सवाल
और ऊपर से धौंस
कि एक बात बताऊँ
साँप कैसा होता है ?
उसके पैर कितने बड़े होते हैं
वो लकड़ी मुँह में रखता है
या हाथ से पकड़ता है ?

when Babaloo got home
he hounded his mom
with endless questions
"can you tell me
what a snake looks like?
how big are its legs?
does it carry sticks in its mouth
or does it pick them up with its hands?"

निगाह में रखी हुई

निगाह में रखी हुई छोटी
शरीर के अँधेरे में बड़ी हो रही है

उसका एक पैर घर की अच्छाई में
दूसरा
बाहर की बुराई में डगमगा रहा है

घर के बड़े 'छोटी कुछ नहीं जानती'
का फायदा उठा रहे हैं

हर शंका के साथ फरार
हर सपने के साथ
बड़ी होकर लौटती

दया, प्यार, निगाह
छोटी के चारों ओर
बहुत-सी गड़बड़ है

पर कोई नहीं जानता
यहाँ तक कि कभी-कभी छोटी भी नहीं
कि चोर उसे किस समय चुराता है

बन्द दरवाज़ों के भीतर
निगाह के घेरे में चोर
कभी उसका साहस
कभी उसका डर बन जाता है
सबके बीच

मन !
तेरी सवारी के लिए
स्कूल ज़रूरी नहीं है
तू कितना ही दौड़े तेरे खुर नहीं फटते

The Girl in Plain Sight

the little girl
is growing up in plain sight
in the body's darkness

half inside the house's goodness
half trembling in the evil
outside

the adults at home
repeat the saying
"the little girl doesn't know a thing"

she flees from every doubt
she returns from every dream
a little bit wiser

blessings, love, attention ...
but all around her
is chaos

no one knows
sometimes not even the little girl
when the thief will come to steal her

inside the locked doors
the thief
in plain sight
can make her bold
or scared
and everyone sees

O mind!
you don't need school to race ahead

जो जहाँ नहीं
छोटी उसको वहाँ देखती है
जैसे कि पिता और पिता के चेहरे में से
कौन पिता है ?

वो हाथी कहाँ है
ब्लाउज़ की बाँह में जिसकी सूँड
माँ का हाथ बन जाती है ?

कमरे-सहित निगाह में रखी हुई
छोटी की हरेक चीज़ बदल रही है
उसके कमरे से एक सड़क निकलती है
पेड़ जिस पर
बूढ़ों की तरह झुके
बगीचे की ओर पीठ फेरे खड़े हैं

खिड़की से बाहर
एक नदी निकलती है
जिसने सिकुड़कर छोटी को रास्ता दिया
और फसलों के बीच से
वह बिल्ली की तरह गुज़रती है

वहाँ उसकी दोस्ती
एक ऐसे दरख़्त से है
जिसके पीछे दो छिप सकते हैं
कोई-से दो नहीं
बल्कि एक वह ख़ुद
और एक जो वह ख़ुद नहीं है ।

no matter how far you run
your hooves will never break

the little girl can see
invisible things
she can tell the difference
between dad and dad's face

where is that elephant
whose trunk pokes out of the blouse's arm
to become mom's hand?

in plain sight of everyone in the room
everything about the little girl is changing
a road extends from her room
where trees
are standing bent like old folks
with their backs toward the gardens

outside the window
a river pulls the little girl aside
to show her the way
and she passes between harvests
like a cat

there she's friends
with the sort of tree
that two can hide behind
not two people
but the one
and the one that is not the one

शब्दोत्सव

सड़क के धनुषाकार एकान्त में
चाँदनी
पत्थर चाट रही है
गुर्राती
किल्ली के आस-पास

ऋतुओं के रस से
कड़ी टहनियाँ
कठोर सहवास को
बाहर ला रही हैं

वे शब्द
सुबह दिखायी देंगे
जिन्हें मैं पाना चाहता हूँ
किसी ठोस घटना के भीतर ।

Wordplay

in the glittering solitude of the street
moonlight
licks the stone
next to
the hissing cat

the thick branches
draw
harsh carnality
from the sweetness of the seasons

in the morning
the words I'm looking for
will appear
in some pure act

उस दिन का जंगल

पिछले पतझर में
हम कितने रोशन थे
जैसे उजाले के दो पेड़

घास बड़ी होती है
तो आपस में दोस्त हो जाती है
पेड़ बड़े होते हैं
तो अकेले हो जाते हैं
(अपने-आपमें उलझे हुए)

पुराने पेड़ों के सान्निध्य में
चिड़िया के घोंसले थे
पुराने पानी में
नये पानी के घुसने का शोर था

आसमान थोड़े-से बादलों के पीछे
पूरा छिपा हुआ था
और हम दो पेजों की तरह
चिपके हुए थे

(समय हमारे बीच
चाकू की तरह नहीं घुसा था)

हमारे चारों ओर
हज़ारों वर्ष पुराना जंगल था
देखकर
जिसने महसूस किया
आनेवाला वसन्त

The Forest That Day

grass grows tall
and embraces other grass
trees grow tall
and draw apart
(entangled in each other's canopies)

and so
last autumn
we glowed
like two radiant trees

in the old trees
there were birds' nests
in the old water
there is the sound of new water

the sky was completely hidden
behind the clouds
and we were stuck together
like pages in a book

(time hadn't yet slipped in
like a pocketknife to split us apart)

looking all around us
the forest that had been there
for a thousand years
could sense
the coming spring

दूर
उस दिन वह ऐसा जगा
हमारे लावण्य-भरे चेहरे खाकर
कि रातों-रात
अपनी खाल का रंग बदलने लगा ।

far away
something was awakened that day
that tasted the sweat on our faces
that in the darkest hour of the night
would change form

स्वप्रदण्ड

बादलों को चीरकर कई सपने तोड़े
फूलों की आँख में पड़ी
धूल तक निकाली

कुछ घायल सपनों का
जवाब तलब किया
कि घोड़े दौड़ाते क्यों आते थे
हमारी नींद के क्षेत्र में ?

क्यों खोद-खोदकर निकालते थे
मन में गड़ी हुई औरतें
फिर हमसे कहते इनसे बात करो

जिस क्षण मन में गड़ी औरतें
सचमुच हमारे साथ हो गयीं
सपने कहीं खो गये

इच्छाओं के इलाके में
जैसे और जितने हम थे
उन्हीं को खोजते भटके

पर उन्होंने बच्चों के ख़ून में
ज्यों ही हमारा ख़ून देखा
तो उनको दिखायी देने लगे सपने

हमको दिखायी दिये
महज़ बच्चे ।

Nightmares

you ripped through the clouds
and tore apart my dreams
you sucked out the dust
fallen into the eyes of flowers

I wanted answers
for my wounded dreams
why did you come into our sleep
on galloping horses?

why did you keep digging up
imaginary women
then tell us to talk to them

then when these imaginary women
came into our real lives
the dreams collapsed

in the land of our desires
you led astray
all those who were like us

but when you saw our blood
in the children's blood
that's when they began to dream

all we saw
were children

मातृमुख

रात के बारह पैंतीस पर
आस-पास कोई ऋतु नहीं है
अँधेरे के पंजे से छूटी हुई कोई ऋतु

एक ठण्ड है
दरवाज़ों, खिड़कियों से टकरायी हुई
जो फेफड़ों में धँसकर
रहने की प्रार्थना से
मेरा एक-एक रोम खट-खटा रही है

मेरे एक-एक रन्ध्र पर कब्ज़ा करके
जो बता रही है
कि एक तारीख किस तरह बीतती है
और दूसरी तक आदमी
किस तरह बदल जाता है

करोड़ों तारे
मेरी पहुँच से दूर बिखरे हुए हैं
रात के प्रसूतिघर में

फेफड़ों के किवाड़ पर खड़ी हुई
आवारा ठण्ड का जकड़ा
क्या मैं माँ को याद कर सकता हूँ ?
जिसकी मौत चेचक से हुई थी

पेड़ सीटियाँ बजा रहे हैं
इतने अकेले में
ये किस्से गुण्डई करेंगे ?

क्या मुझसे ?
क्योंकि मेरे दिमाग में
इस वक्त मेरी माँ है

My Mother's Face

at a quarter till one in the morning
there's no way to tell what season it is
the season has been stolen by the talons of the night

rapping on doors and windows
the cold
enters my lungs
asking humbly for a place to stay
it makes me shiver from head to toe

it lays siege to my body's every pore
telling me
how one age passes
and how a person will change
over time

millions of stars
lie scattered beyond my grasp
in the night's womb

the wandering cold
raps against my lungs' doors
can I remember my mom
dead years ago from smallpox?

the trees are whistling
who are they going to rob
in this utter desolation?

me?
because at this moment
I'm thinking about
my mom

मैं हज़ारों चेहरों को देखकर
अन्दाज़ लगा सकता हूँ
कि चेचक ने कैसे उसके चेहरे की
गोड़ाई की होगी

रात के चेहरे पर तारे देखकर
क्यों मेरे मन में
एक तस्वीर बन रही है ?
मुझे उसके चेहरे पर पड़े
काले बालों की याद
केवल काले बालों की याद
मेरे लिए माँ का चेहरा है

इन्तज़ार हज़ार साल पहले से
आदमी को गन्दा कर रहा है

मुझे भी इन्तज़ार है
कि कभी माँ के चेचकग्रस्त चेहरे की
रचना कर सकूँगा

रात के बारह पैंतीस को
क्या मैं कह सकता हूँ 'इस समय' ?

इस समय मेरे आस-पास
उस समय के चेहरे पर पड़े वे बाल हैं
जिनकी याद और जिनका रंग
फेफड़ों की धुन्ध में
थोड़ा-सा वात्सल्य है

रात के बारह पैंतीस पर
क्या मैं किसी चीज़ को
माँ की तरह जान सकता हूँ ?

कफन जिसको, धोती की तरह पहना दिया गया
मिट्टी का हिस्सा बनने से पहले
वह कोख थी

having seen thousands of faces
I can guess
how smallpox would have ravaged
her face

looking at the stars in the night sky
why is it that one image
comes to mind?
the memory of her black hair
covering her face
the memory of black hair
all I remember of my mom's face
is her black hair

waiting for thousands of years
has ruined people

I'm also waiting
to remember
my mom's smallpox-scarred face

at a quarter till one in the morning
can I say "now"?

now all around me
is the black hair that once covered her face
the traces
in the hazy air of my lungs
of parental love

at a quarter till one in the morning
can I know anything
anything like my mom?

like a dhoti
the shroud was wrapped around her

कभी जिसकी वजह से मैं संसार में आया

तब से घर के भीतर का अँधेरा
माँ का चेहरा है
जो रात-भर गालों से सटा
— जागता रहता है

माँ के बालों से टपकती
यह चेचकमुखी रात
धीरे-धीरे प्रशान्त
समुद्र तक चली गयी है

ऐ मेरी मातृमुखी रात !
इस बिगड़ैल अन्धकार को समझाओ
मेरी तरह यह भी तुम्हारा ही पुत्र है
कभी न कभी
तुमने इसे अपने बालों से जन्मा था

अगर मैं तुम्हें याद कर रहा हूँ
तो यह सीटियाँ न बजाये ।

then she was returned to the earth
I came into the world
from her womb

since then the darkness inside the house
is my mom's face
pressed against my cheeks
it never leaves me

this pockmarked night
full of my mom's hair
has slowly slipped toward
the quiet ocean

O maternal night!
explain to this angry darkness
that just as I am your son
it too is your son
your hair gave birth to it

if this is you I'm remembering
then I won't ask for more

आत्मकारा

बरसती रात के
आर-पार फँसे हुए हैं हम

न हमारे पास छाता है
न लाठी । न लालटेन
न सिर पर टोपी
न पैरों के नीचे रास्ता
अपने ही क्रोध में
निष्कवच फँसे हुए हैं हम

अखण्ड रात की हवा में
जंजीर खणमणा रही है
कुछ पता नहीं चल रहा
हम बँधे हुए हैं या कि खुल्ला ?

यात्रा के भ्रम में
पुराने प्रसंग को कुरेदकर
दिमाग के भीतर
हमने एक सुरंग बनायी
और ऐसे मौके पर
संसार के प्रतिबिम्ब के पीछे लुक गये

समुद्रतटों से लेकर
शिखरों तक फैले हुए
जमीन के एक बहुत बड़े हिस्से ने
हमको आवाज़ दी
'मैं रहा तुम्हारा देश
कारखाने से लेकर कब्र तक
कानून से लेकर कारागार तक
कई चीज़ों के काम आ सकता हूँ'

Prison of the Soul

throughout the monsoon night
we're trapped

we don't have an umbrella
or club or lantern
or hat for our head
or path beneath our feet
we're trapped in our anger
without anything
to fend it off

in the endless night's wind
the fetters rattle
can you tell
whether we're in chains
or free?

on the disorienting journey
digging up old loves
we cut a tunnel
through our minds
and then
disappeared behind the world's reflection

from the ocean coasts
to the tops of mountains
a large swath of the earth
spoke to us
I'm still your country
from factories to graves
from laws to prisons
I can serve many purposes

हम एक हाथ उठाते हैं
और अँधेरे में उसके लिए जगह बन जाती है
फिर कभी वह हाथ
वापस आकर हमसे नहीं मिलता
फिर कभी वह हाथ
हमारे मुँह तक नहीं आता

बरसती रात के आर-पार
तमाम दिन घाव की तरह चमक रहे हैं
कुछ पता नहीं चल रहा
हम बँधे हैं या कि खुल्ला ?

we raise a hand
and space is carved out in the darkness for it
but then this hand
will never return to us
this hand
will no longer feed us

throughout the monsoon night
all the days sparkle like wounds
and it's impossible to say
whether we're in chains or free

बच्चे-३

बच्चा पैदा होने का मतलब है
फिर एक आदमी खतरे में पड़ा

याने कि ख़ून
अब
बीज और जंगल
और आबादी के बहाने
पकड़ में आ गया है

एक बच्चा पैदा होने का मतलब
कि एक आदमी जवान होगा
लड़ेगा
और न्याय जिनका स्वार्थ है
उनको पराजित करेगा

पराजित करेगा
मौत के उन ताकतवर पंजों को भी
जो अपने साथ सोते-सोते उगते हैं
और गर्दन को इसलिए दुलराते हैं
क्योंकि वह दबोचनी है

इसलिए बच्चा होने की घटना
(बच्चे के वास्ते जो कि बड़ी बात नहीं है)
बेचैन कर देती है
और मेरी इस लम्बी साँस का मतलब है
कि फिर एक आदमी
खतरे में पड़ा

एक बच्चा । एक दूसरा बच्चा
फिर एक तीसरा बच्चा
याने ये 'बच्चा लोग'
आनेवाले दिनों के
'मार तमाम आदमी लोग हैं'

Children (III)

the meaning of having a child
is that another person's life is in danger

meaning that
now
on the excuse
of a seed and a forest
and a people
blood will be shed

the meaning of having a child
is that a young person
will fight
and justice will defeat
self-interests

and will defeat
the powerful clutches of death as well
that sleeping with justice awakes
and caresses the neck
because soon the neck
must be strangled

being a child
(which isn't in any way odd for children)
makes everyone uneasy
and the meaning of my sighs
is that now someone's
life is in danger

one child then a second child
then a third child
meaning these children

तमाम आदमी लोग
पहले 'बच्चा' थे
और जब बड़े हुए तो उन्होंने कहा
कि — 'बच्चे बेवकूफ होते हैं'

बच्चे जो भी होते हों
बड़े होते ही
बच्चों के खिलाफ हो जाते हैं
(इस तरह
बेवकूफ लोग बड़े होते रहे)

एक जवान या बूढ़ा आदमी
बचपना कर सकता है
लेकिन एक बच्चा वही करता है
जो उसे करना चाहिए

मसलन कि बचपना करने के लिए
पहले
बचपन के कत्ल से
गुज़रना पड़ता है

एक बच्चा 'एक आदमी' है
दूसरा बच्चा 'दूसरा आदमी'
बचपन का एक
बचपन के दूसरे से
बदला लेना चाहता है

क्योंकि दोनों ने
अपने बचपन को
एकसाथ खत्म किया था

याने जब वे बचपन को
खत्म करके लौटे
तो काफी खूनी हो छूके थे

अब उन्हें लड़ने के लिए

in the days to come
will be adults

all adults
were once children
and once they become adults
they say *kids are fools*

whatever children are
as soon as they grow up
they turn against children
(this is how
fools are born)

a young or an old man
can act like a child
but a child acts
exactly like a child should act

meaning
in order to act like a child
first
you must have already
killed childhood

one child is one man
another child is another man
the childhood of the one
wants to exchange childhoods
with the other

because both
put an end to their childhoods
at the same time

meaning

कई ऐसे मैदानों की तलाश है
जिन्हें नदियों ने न बनाया हो
मगर जहाँ उनका बहना
दृश्य बदलने के लिए
बहुत ज़रूरी है ।

by the time the men returned home
from killing childhood
a lot of blood had already been shed

now they're looking
for fields to fight in
that were not made by rivers
but where the course of rivers
is desperately needed
to change the world

विदा

जब मैं वापस आया
जितना मैं चाहता था उतना नहीं
बल्कि तुमने जितना मुझे वापस किया
तो उतना नहीं था
जितनी सम्भावना थी

तुम्हारे शब्द यहाँ मँडरा रहे हैं
तुम्हें विदा कर पाना
बहुत मुश्किल है

विदा करने में
विदा पाया हुआ
अगर मैं जल्दी-जल्दी कदम रखू
और सौ साल वहाँ पर खत्म हों
जहाँ पर
इस छोटे-से पौधे में
फूल और फल है

उतनी दूरी तक जो एक ऊँचाई हैं
बिना व्यवधान की
तुम्हें विदा करने के बाद
जब में वापस आया तो मुझमें थी

अब एक बिल्कुल नया आदमी हूँ
विदा करने में विदा पाया हुआ
कच्चे फलों की तरह
झुकना सीखता हुआ
छाया में जिसकी बेंत उठाये
पहले ही बच्चे खड़े हैं

ये पेड़ जब पकेगा
बड़ी तड़ातड़ होगी ।

Goodbye

when I came back
I didn't get as much as I wanted
what you gave back to me
wasn't as much
as I'd expected

here your words are filling the air
leaving you
is hard

in saying goodbye
I found a way to leave
if I walked away quickly
and one hundred years passed
in this place where
on this little tree
are flowers and fruit

after having left you
when I came back
inside me was endless
unbroken distance

now I'm a completely new person
in saying goodbye
I found a way to leave
like raw fruit
I learned to bend low
in the shadows when a cane is raised
where once children were standing

when this tree matures
there will be the loud sound of snapping

बलदेव खटिक

रात ; चिथड़ा खाती गाय के जबड़े में
धीरे-धीरे गायब हो रही थी
यह उसका अन्तिम छोर था
जिस पर एक बटन चमक रहा था

तभी हमारे गाँव के आकाश में
अचानक लोगों ने एक दरार देखी
सड़क से गाँव पर रौशनी फेंकती
यह पुलिस की गाड़ी थी

लेकिन यह इतना पैना उजाला नहीं था
कि अँधेरे के भीतर दुबके अँधेरे में
कुछ आँखें, कुछ हाथ, कुछ पाँव चमक उठें

वे भड़भड़ाकर उतरे
और रँगतू के घर की ओर दौड़े
उनकी दुरुस्त और निर्विघ्न दौड़ बताती थी
कि हमारे गाँव की चल ख़राब हो गयी है
उनकी पोशाक

हमारे गाँव के कुत्तों तक के लिए
अपरिचित थी

जिसके चिथड़े न पहने हुए हों
हमारे गाँव की गरीब जनता के कुत्ते हैं
सभ्य और अजनबी पोशाकों के दुश्मन
लेकिन चार जोड़ी
पुलिस के बूटों में
उन्हें बैल के चमड़े की गंध नहीं आ रही थी
उनके पुलिसपैर
एक लाइन में
जैसे जलओद उछल रहे थे

Baldev Khatik

night—like a rag
in the jaws of a cow
slowly disappearing
at its end a shiny button

then in the sky above our village
suddenly a crack opened
and light from the road hit the village
it was a police car

but the light wasn't so bright
that in the drowned darkness
within the darkness
you couldn't make out eyes
hands or feet

screaming and shouting
they descended from the road
running in the direction of Rangtu's house
their firm steady strides made us feel
how backward our village was
even our dogs didn't recognize their uniforms

our dogs would attack anyone
who wasn't wearing rags
these were the dogs of the poor villagers
the enemies of city fashion
the four pairs of police boots
didn't smell like the hides of water buffaloes
the policemen in a row
their feet rising and falling steadily
like water in a fountain

क्योंकि ऐसे मौके पर
जो जिसके पास है
उसका उपयोग ज़रूरी हो जाता है
इसलिए कुत्ते भौंक रहे थे

जो रँगतू
कल राशन लूटने में शरीक था
उनके पास उसके नाम का वारण्ट
उसके परिवार ने रात भरपेट खाया है
भूख-भर अन्न के नशे में
अपने देश का एक मामूली घर भी
आरामगाह बना हुआ है
(वैसे उसे घर कहना भी
खामोखा जिन्हें घर कहते हैं
उनकी बढ़िया छतों पर घास उगा देना है)

करीब-करीब अपनी इच्छाओं की मुट्ठी खोलकर
इस समय तक वे सोये हुए हैं

अपनी लात में ताकत पैदा करके
उन्होंने उसे बूट से उठाया
और तुरंत उसके हाथ बाँध दिये
(वे हाथ जो बड़ी-बड़ी इमारतों पर
पलस्तर की तरह चिपके हुए हैं)
फिर थोड़ा बचे हुए अनाज के साथ
उसे शहर ले गये
जहाँ आदमी के लिए
जेल और पोस्टमार्टम की पूरी व्यवस्था है

पुलिसवालों पर आदमियों की आँखें थीं
इसलिए रँगतू की नंगी औरत
बाहर नहीं आ सकी
लेकिन भीतर
बच्चे उसके शरीर से पहनावे की तरह चिपके हुए थे

on occasions like these
you have to put to use
whatever you have
and so the dogs were barking

now they had an arrest warrant for Rangtu
who had been looting rations
last night his family stuffed themselves
desperate for anything they could get their hands on
for one night an ordinary house in our country
was made into a pleasure palace
(but even to call it a house is wrong
it wasn't as good as that)

up to this point
they were still dreaming their pleasant dreams

the officers drew up their strength
and kicked Rangtu awake
they immediately cuffed him
(his hands fastened together
like plaster on the side of a building)
took what of the grain remained
then took him to the city
where there are the proper facilities
for jailing a man and performing his postmortem

the villagers were staring at the police
so Rangtu's naked wife
couldn't come outside
inside
her kids clung to her
like clothes

then morning was shuddering
down the car's engine

यह सुबह थी
गाड़ी के इंजन पर थरथराती हुई
अँधेरे के भीतर दुबके हुए अँधेरे में
बीबी-बच्चों के लिए लड़ता हुआ रँगतू
पहली बार गाड़ी पर "फ्री" चढ़ रहा था

यह एक ऐसा वक्त था
जब वनस्पति
केवल घी के डिब्बे का मतलब था
और कहीं भी कोई शब्द अपनी क्रीज़ में नहीं था

शब्द जो कि दाल और भात हैं
शब्द जो कि रोटी और साग हैं
नहीं-नहीं ; शब्द इतनी बड़ी चीज़ नहीं है
शब्द केवल रोटी पर रखे हुए नमक के कण हैं
शब्द जो लार बनाते हैं
इस वक्त कहाँ से लाये जायें ऐसे शब्द
जो हलफ़नामा बन सकें
जो तरफ़दारी कर सकें

पुलिस की गाड़ी में उसकी शब्दहीन आत्मा
एक नंगे पेड़ की तरह है
जिस पर थाने पहुंचने से पहले
कई हज़ार घमौरियां फूट पड़ेंगी
कई हज़ार लाल घमौरियों में बंद पत्ते
निशान की तरह बाहर उभर आएंगे
भाषा अचानक सारे शरीर में फल पड़ेंगी
और कई हज़ार जीभों से बोलता हुआ
वह बरी हो जायेगा

अपनी जड़ों के सहारे
अपनी मिट्टी में उतरा हुआ रँगतू
न पेड़ है । न पत्ता है । न हवा है
अँधेरे के भीतर दुबका हुआ अँधेरे का कीड़ा भी नहीं
शब्द भी नहीं

in the darkness drowned within the darkness
and Rangtu
who had been fighting for his wife and kids
was riding for "free" in a car for the first time

this was during the years
when Vanaspati meant only a tub of ghee
and there wasn't a single word
that stood sharp and ready for the day

"lentils" and "rice" are words
"bread" and "spinach" are words
no, no—words aren't such important things
words are just flecks of salt on bread
words cause your mouth to water
now where can you find words
that can be sworn statements
that can provide testimony?

in the car on the way to the police station
his mute soul is like a leafless tree
on whose branches thousands of buds will open
inside thousands of red buds the leaves
that will burst forth in prickly heat
his entire body will erupt in words
and speaking with a thousand tongues
he will give them what they want

holding onto his roots
descending into his soil
Rangtu isn't a tree or a leaf or the wind
not even an insect of the darkness drowning in the darkness
not even a word

रँगतू एक अकेले आदमी का दर्द है
और अकेला आदमी अपराधी होता है
सवालों के जत्थों से भरा हुआ अकेला आदमी
एक दुर्घटना होता है

थाने पहुँचते ही
गाड़ी से उतरते हुए रँगतू ने
थोड़ा देर के लिए खुद को बड़ा आदमी महसूस किया
ड्राइवर ने गाड़ी का डाला खोला
और वह सिपाहियों की ही तरह कूदता हुआ
ज़मीन पर खड़ा हो गया

तभी एक सिपाही को (जो रास्ते-भर बीड़ी पीता रहा)
घर से आया हुआ तर दिया गया
तार पर उसकी माँ बीमार थी
लेकिन उसे शाम तक छुट्टी नहीं मिली

पक्का 'जेल आडर' बनवाने तक
वह रँगतू को, रस्सा पकड़े हुए
एक कमरे से दूसरे कमरे में ले जाता रहा
तीन गिलास चाय
और बावन पैसे की बीड़ी के धोरे पहुँचने के बाद
जिस समय झण्डा उतरने का गजर बज रहा था
उस समय रँगतू को कम्बल, कोठरी और नंबर मिल रहा था
(लेकिन सिपाही की माँ
जेब में मुड़े हुए तार पर छटपटा रही थी)

जब तीसरे दिन छुट्टी पर
वह अपने गाँव पहुँचा तो उसकी माँ
सुई की नोक पर
अभी झड़ पड़नेवाली
पानी की बूँद की तरह इन्तज़ार कर रही थी

वह भागा-भागा जिला अस्पताल गया
एम्बुलेंस माँगी

Rangtu is one man's pain
because when alone one man is a criminal
when alone one man full of questions
is an accident waiting to happen

at the station
while getting out of the police car
Rangtu felt like an important person for a second
the driver opened the back gate
and he jumped out like cops do

then one police officer
(the one who had been smoking bidis the whole way)
was handed a cable from home
saying his mom was sick
but he was on duty until late

while the official charge sheet was being drawn up
the officer led Rangtu by a rope
from one room to another
after three glasses of chai
and half a rupee worth of bidis
it was time to lower the flag in the evening
the officer assigned Rangtu a blanket cell and number
(while his mom writhed in the crumpled-up telegram
in his pocket)

three days later
when the cop got back to his village
his mom was barely hanging on
like a drop of water
dangling from the tip of a needle

he ran straight to the district hospital
asking to use the broken-down ambulance

भाँग के पौधों के बीच जो ख़राब खड़ी थी
धतूरा जिसके इंजन से बड़ा हो गया था

कई पुरानी लाशों को लाँघते हुए
उसने चारों ओर अपना दिमाग दौड़ाया
और जब बड़ी मुश्किल से एक विचार
उसकी पकड़ में आया
तो वह लपककर पास ही थाने में गया

क्योंकि आजकल केवल आदमी होना
न्यायसंगत नहीं है
इसलिए उसने बताया कि मैं भी पुलिस विभाग का
आदमी हूँ
माँ को अस्पताल लाने के लिए
थोड़ा पुलिसगाड़ी दे दीजिए

उन्होंने कहा
पुलिस की गाड़ी अपराधियों को पकड़ने के लिए है
घर पर मरो या अस्पताल में मरो
सड़क पर मरो या शमशानघाट पर पहुँचकर मरो
मरना कहीं भी अपराध नहीं है

और फिर तुम्हारी माँ का
हमारे पास कोई वारण्ट नहीं जो हम गाड़ी भेज दें
आखिर मरनेवाले को कौन पकड़ सकता है
अक्सर हमारे पकड़े हुए भी मर जाते हैं

जब शाम को एक दवा की शीशी और कुछ गोलियाँ लेकर
वह घर आया
तो उसने अपनी माँ को मरा हुआ पाया
संसार से यह फरारी किस अपराध से बचती है ?

अभावों की इस आज़ाद कहानी में
क्या इसी तरह होती है मुक्ति ?

parked in the hemp plants
a thornapple bush growing from its engine block

amid the hospital's dead
he wracked his brains
finally he thought of something
and he set off running for the nearby police station

because today simply being human
isn't good enough
he told them he was also a cop
please give me a police car
so I can take my mom to the hospital

they said
police vehicles are for catching criminals
die at home or the hospital
die on the street or the cremation ghat
wherever you die it's still not a crime

add to that
since there's no warrant out for your mom
we can't send a car
after all who can stop people bent on dying
we see it often enough even in the station

when he got back home that evening
medicine and pills in hand
his mom was already dead
from what crime does fleeing from the world save us?

in this tale of the have-nots
is this really how spiritual liberation is achieved?

आखिर बढ़ाई हुई छुट्टियों में
जब उसने अपनी माँ को स्वर्ग पहुँचा दिया
तब वह फिर थाना बिजनौर में लौट आया

वह विरक्त होना चाहता था
लेकिन अपना भविष्य उसे
भीतर-ही-भीतर ठग रहा था
कर्मकाण्ड की सारी कमज़ोरी को ढकता हुआ
उसका उस्तराफिरा सर
किसी फिल्मी गुण्डे का सिर लग रहा था

फिल्मवालों को जब गुण्डे और हत्यारे
दिखाने होते हैं
तो वे अभिनेता पर आम आदमी को मेकप कर देते हैं

बात दूसरी ओर चली जायेगी
क्योंकि इस बात को कान और जुबान की तलाश है
इसलिए मैं आपको
फिर से थाना बिजनौर ले चलता हूँ
जहाँ अपना घुटा हुआ सिर लेकर
वह सिपाही इस समय संतरी-ड्यूटी पर है

उसकी छाती पर गोलियों का पट्टा है
उसके हाथ में एक बंदूक है
उसे नहीं मालूम वह किसकी रक्षा कर रहा है
(मेरी समझ से वह केवल टहल रहा है)

क्या वह संसार की अपराध से रक्षा कर रहा है ?
क्या वह इस देश को बिगड़ने से बचा रहा है ?
भीतर एक कमरे में
अपने गंदे लेकिन वरिष्ठ दाँतों को लेकर
दीवान बैठा है
रोज़नामचे पर हाथ रखे हुए
जैसे वह शहर की पीठ हो

एक मार खाया हुआ आदमी चिंचियाता है

while on extended leave
he sent his mom off to heaven
then returned to the Bijnor Police Station

he didn't want his feelings to show
but his future
was quietly slipping away
he kept silent about how upset the funeral had made him
he shaved his head to show his grief
he looked like someone in a gangster film

when film directors want scenes with gangsters and guns
they gussy up actors to make them look like normal people

now let's go back
to the Bijnor Police Station
where that police officer with his shaven head
is stationed on guard duty

he's wearing a bulletproof vest
he's carrying a rifle
he doesn't know who he's guarding
(it seems like he's just pacing back and forth)

is he protecting someone against the unjust world?
is he saving the country from going to ruin?
inside a room
his commanding officer
is seated
stained teeth showing his years
his hands gathered on top of the logbook
make it look like he's holding up the city

a battered and bruised man screams
my wallet was stolen
my girl's photo is in there

मेरा बटुआ छिन गया
उसमें मेरी लड़की का फोटो भी था
वे उससे बलात्कार करेंगे
वे उसे मार डालेंगे
देखिए, मुझे कितनी चोटें आयी हैं
मेरा दर्द — दर्ज करो
इस मटीले काग़ज़ पर मेरा दर्द — दर्ज करो

अपने होंठों पर मुर्दा दिन को ज़िंदा करते हुए
दीवान कहता है
किस कलम से करूँ ?
चांदी की कलम से करूँ ? सोने की कलम से करूँ
कि लकड़ी की कलम से करूँ ?

मार खाया हुआ आदमी रिरियाता है
कि कानून की कलम से करो

कानून की कलम लड़की की होती है
दीवान कहता है — कल आना
मगर अपना गबाह भी साथ लाना
और किसी डाक्टर से यह भी लिखवा लाना
कि तुमने मार खायी-ही-खायी है ...

बाहर सन्तरी-ड्यूटी पर खड़ा बलदेव खटिक
जिसका सिर मुंडा हुआ है
जिसकी माँ बिना दवाई के मर गयी थी
सब सुन रहा है
(थाने की बड़ी घड़ी सुधाकर
घड़ीसाज़ फाटक से बाहर जा रहा है)

अचानक सामने खड़े नीम के पेड़ पर
उतरते शाम के कौवों से बलदेव खटिक कहता है
— 'थ्थम'
मगर वे नहीं रुकते
वह धड़ाधड़ फायर करता है
बन्दूक के बट को थाने की दीवार से मारकर

they'll rape her
they'll beat her
look, look at my wounds
my pain
record my pain in your silly book!

with his lips
breathing life back into the dead day
the commanding officer says
what pen should I use? the silver one?
the gold one? the wood one?

the battered and bruised man sobs
use the pen of justice!

the commanding officer says
the pen of justice is the wooden one
come back tomorrow
bring your witness too
and get a doctor to write a note
saying how you've been beaten up ...

outside Baldev Khatik is on guard duty
his head shaven for
his mom who died without ever getting medicine
he's listening to everything inside
(he corrects the police station's big clock
and steps outside the main gate)

to the crows in the neem tree
suddenly Baldev Khatik says *quiet!*
but they don't stop
and so he fires his rifle
he smashes its butt against the police station wall
it breaks
and he races down the stairs

तोड़ देता है
और सीढ़ियां उतरकर
सड़क पर मरे हुए कौवों को लाँघकर
फरार हो जाता है

(थाने की बगल में उस समय सिनेमाघर के भीतर
पर्दे पर एक ऐक्टर प्यार कर रहा था)

अब तक वह संतरी था
अब वह बलदेव खटिक है
'माँ की चूत इस नौकरी की' कहकर वह
माँ, माँ, माँ चिल्लाता हुआ
सीधा हमारे गाँव में घुस आया

उसके सर पर टोपी नहीं है
कमीज़ हाफपैंट से बाहर आ गयी है
वह हरेक औरत से पूछता है तुमको क्या बीमारी है ?
अस्पताल तक पैदल चलो । गाड़ी ख़राब है

बच्चों से कहता है लाओ मेरी लकड़ी का कलम
मैं फैसला लिख दूँ

किसी की बीमारी सुने बगैर
किसी के पास एक क्षण रुके बगैर
किसी को कोई फैसला दिए बगैर
वह दौड़ता हुआ आया
और रँगतू की झोपड़ी में
बेहोश होकर गिर पड़ा

(झोपड़ी का दरवाज़ा खुला हुआ था
रँगतू राशनवाले मामले में जेल चला गया था
और उसकी औरत भी बच्चों समेत
वहाँ नहीं थी
मगर किसी ने भी उन्हें कहीं जाते नहीं देखा था
भीतर से नींद में पूंछ झुकाये हुए
एक कुत्ता निकला और अगली गली में मुड़ गया)

steps over the dead crows
and flees amid the lengthening shadows of the evening

(just then inside the movie theater
next to the police station there was an actor
falling in love)

he was a guard up till now
now he's Baldev Khatik
he yelled *this job can go fuck itself!*
and crying *mom! mom! mom!*
he came straight
to our village

he isn't wearing a hat
his shirt is no longer tucked into his police shorts
he asks every woman *what's wrong? are you sick?*
let's walk to the hospital
the car's broken down

he tells all the kids
bring my wooden pen
I'll bring you justice

without caring about anyone's illness
without stopping for a second anywhere
without bringing any justice
he came running
and collapsed unconscious
in Rangtu's hut

(the hut's door was open
Rangtu had been put in jail for stealing rations
and his wife and kids weren't there
although no one had seen them leave
from inside a sleepy dog

सुबह होनेवाली है
लेकिन रात अब भी मौजूद है
रात उस वक़्त भी मौजूद रहेगी
जब लोग दोपहर को ढलते हुए देख रहे होंगे

हर घर को अपने दर्द में लपेटती
दरवाज़ों की संधों को थोड़ा और चौड़ा करती हुई
रात ब्यानेवाली है
चिड़ियों और कौवों और कुत्तों के सामूहिक शोर में
पत्तियां थरथरानेवाली हैं ...

तभी हमारे गाँव के आकाश में
अचानक लोगों ने एक दरार देखी
सड़क से रोशनी फेंकती हुई
फिर यह पुलिस की गाड़ी थी

राख की तरह झरती सुबह में
चमकती हुई कुत्तों की भौंक के बीच
बीड़ी पीते हुए वे उतरे
सम्बन्धों की वीरानगी में
उनके साधारण चहेरों पर
घरेलु थपेड़ों की गहरी शिनाख्त है
टट्टी फिरते हुए बच्चे हैं । फोड़े हैं
चूल्हे पर चढ़ा हुआ खदबदाता पानी है
भात के भपारे हैं

वे उतरे और रँगतू की झोंपड़ी से
उस पागल सिपाही को बांधकर ले गये
पहले उन्होंने उसके सरकारी कपड़े उतरे
क्योंकि अपराधी नहीं होती

यह अलग बात है कि हथकड़ी और सज़ा
इन दोनों में से
आम आदमी के लिए सरकार क्या होती है ?

with its tail tucked between its legs
came out and turned into the next alley)

it's almost dawn
but night persists
night will remain
even while everyone's watching the afternoon end

every house will be wrapped in its own pain
it is almost night
which cracks open doors just a bit wider
and in the clamor of the birds and the crows and the dogs
the leaves are about to start trembling …

then above our village
suddenly people saw something
a light appeared on the road
it was a police car

morning came in a shower of embers
and amid the barking of crazed dogs
they descended from the road smoking bidis
hardened by their lot
their plain faces
telling the stories of household abuse
of kids shitting down their legs
of blisters
of water simmering on the stove
of the steam of cooked rice

they descended from the road to Rangtu's hut
where they cuffed the crazy police officer
and took off his police uniform
before taking him away
because the government isn't crazy
the government isn't a criminal

उन्होंने भी उसे हथकड़ी पहना दी
और आम आदमी में तब्दील कर दिया

वह अपने ही गाल पर चांटे मार रहा है
उसके पास न कोई सहमति है और न कोई इंकार
धरती को पीटते हुए
वह अपने ही पैर तोड़ रहा है

फिर भी उसके पागल सिर पर
बाल
आधा इंच बड़े हो गये हैं
उसके लंबे नाखून संसार की धूल से
गन्दे हो रहे हैं
उसके हाथों में अब भी एक आदमी की ताकत
मौजूद है
लेकिन उसे अपने दुश्मन की सही पहचान नहीं है
और उसने गोलियां सही जगह नहीं दागी हैं

अब वह एक कोठरी में बन्द है
और उससे बयालीस नम्बर जूनियर
बाहर एक सन्तरी है
एक खम्भे से दूसरे खम्भे तक टहलता हुआ
चेहरे से ज्यादा जिसके बूट में चमक है
अपनी मुस्तैदी में
जिसका समूचा शरीर
अनुशासन की रग है

उसकी छाती पर भी
गोलियों का एक पट्टा है
सिर पर टोपी है और हाथ में बन्दूक है
मगर यह पहलेवाले सिपाही से कहाँ पर अलग है ?

यह भी अपने देश को
न कहीं पर पाता है
न कहीं पर खोता है
उससे कहा गया है कि हरेक पर शक करो

it's another matter that since then
for the common man
all "government" means
is handcuffs and punishment

they put him in cuffs
and turned him into an ordinary person

he's punching himself in the face
there's no consoling him now
kicking the ground
he's hurting only his own feet

now on his crazy head
his hair
has grown a half inch
his long nails are growing black from the world
he is still as strong
as a person is
but he doesn't know who his enemy is
and his bullets have missed their real targets

now he's locked in a room
outside a guard
junior officer #42
paces from one pole to another
that his boots shine more than his eyes do
shows his eagerness for duty
from head to toe
his body is the epitome of discipline

on his chest
is a bulletproof vest
he's wearing a hat and carrying a rifle
but how is he different from the first guard?

विश्वास केवल दीवान का करो — दरोगा का करो
(उसका निजी कोई विश्वास नहीं)
अब देखना यह है कि
ये कब पागल होता है !

एक अच्छा खासा
काम करता हुआ आदमी
पागल हो जाये
१९७४ की राजनीति में
इसके लिए कोई शब्द नहीं
मैं आपको यकीन दिलाता हूँ
बलदेव खटिक के खानदान में
कोई पागल नहीं था

आप लोग अपनी परवाह करें
अपने बच्चों की जाँच करवायें
यह केवल अफवाह नहीं
(बल्कि जिन्दा होने की नयी शर्त है)
कि देश में कुछ लोग
पेट से ही पागल होकर आ रहे हैं

लेकिन वे जब फायर करेंगे
तो यह तय है कि
इस बार कौवे नहीं मरेंगे ।

about his country
he too doesn't know anything
he was told to doubt everyone
to trust only his commanding officer
and his superiors
(but never to trust himself)
now we will have to wait and see
when he will go crazy too!

a good, hard-working man
went crazy
in the politics of 1974
there's no word for this
but you can trust me
there are no crazy people
in Baldev Khatik's family

everyone look out for yourselves
look after your kids
it's not just a rumor
(it's a new condition of living)
that in this country some people
are going crazy from hunger

but now when they open fire
it's already been settled
this time it won't be crows that die

खेल

बहुत-कुछ अपने-जैसा
जन्मते ही जो एक आदमी
लीलाधर जगूड़ी नहीं था
वह मैं हूँ

मेरा जन्म ही कठोर कारागार है
— जन्म ही कठोर कारागार है
— मैं जन्म से ही कठोर कारागार में हूँ

कैदियों को भी प्यार की ज़रूरत है
ये कब से कहा जा रहा है

पहले यहाँ
मेरे पिता फँसे
— जब मैं आया वे जेलर बन गये

तब से मेरे दायें हाथ का काम
उनके
बायें हाथ का खेल हो गया ।

A Game

so much like me
as soon as he was born that man
who was not Leeladhar Jagoori
was me

my birth alone is a harsh prison
—birth alone is a harsh prison
—since birth itself I've been in a harsh prison

prisoners need love too
for how long has this been said

first it was here
where my father was trapped
—when I was born he was already a jail guard

from then on what was hard for me
was child's play for him

बची हुई पृथ्वी पर

आज का दिन इस घाटी में मेरा दुसरा दिन है
और एक-एक कण की रणगाथा से भरी
समुद्र-सहित तैरती यह पृथ्वी
आती-जाती रोशनी का तट है

ज़मीन की भाषा में ज़मीन को
पानी की भाषा में पानी को
कुछ कहना कितना मुश्किल है
अपनी भाषा में अपने को
कुछ कह भी सकूँ और यहाँ रह भी सकूँ
कितना मुश्किल है

फिर भी हरे टुकड़ों के बीच
इस जगह एक घर होता
स्वाद से भरा,
रोग से बचा
तो सुन्दर कितनी थी यह नदी

'गूँगे खामोश हैं'
ऐसा एकदम नहीं कहा जा सकता
क्योंकि कई गाँवों को
मज़बूत किलों में बदलनेवाले पत्थर
यहाँ इन्तज़ार कर रहे हैं

और आकाश की जीभ बनकर
ताकतवर सन्नाटा
जंगल चखने के बाद
इन्हें चाट रहा है

काई, इन पर उस समय की यादगार है
जो न कोई था, न पत्थर, न जंगल, न नदी

On the Remaining Earth

today in this valley is my tomorrow
and the floating earth with its oceans
full of the war anthems of a thousand million things
is a shore of flickering light

it's so difficult to speak
about the ground in the language of the ground
about water in the language of water
what could I say about myself in my own language
and remain living here
it's so difficult

yet between the green shores
this place is still one "home"
full of pleasure
having escaped disease
how beautiful this river is

the deaf-mute is silent ...
this can never truly be said
because the stones removed
from well-built forts
are waiting here for many villages

and having become the sky's tongue
and having tasted the forests
the powerful silence
is licking these stones

their moss is a souvenir of things from that time
which was not moss not stone not forest not river

जब कि किस मुल्क के ईश्वर का समय
मौत का समय नहीं है ?

सूर्योदय के आस-पास यह नदी है
और नदी के आस-पास यह सूर्योदय ;
नए हैं
क्योंकि पृथ्वी पुरानी

जिस पर एक दिन की लकड़ियाँ
कई दूसरे दिनों का ईंधन हैं
तम्बू के पीछे
एक दूसरे दिन का धुआँ उठ रहा है
सन्नाटे के हाथ पर
जैसे चिलम आ गयी हो

जो चीज़ें, जो बातें
जिन लोगों में अभी नहीं हैं
वे उनके लिए नयी होंगी
अगले साल

अगले साल के पीछे
नहीं दिखायी दे रहा है
जो एक और अगला साल
उससे कहीं ज़्यादा साफ दिखायी दे रहा है
कई वर्ष पुरानी इस जगह पर
मेरा यह दूसरा दिन

अगले क्षण इस दिन की चाय
कहीं नहीं होगी
तीसरे दिन के सामान में से
चौथा दिन बचाना है ।

when was the time of any country's god
not the time of death?

this river is near the sunrise
and this sunrise is near the river
they are new
because the earth is old

where the sticks for one day
are the kindling for days to come
behind the tent
the smoke of another day is rising
in the palm of stillness
as though a chillum has been lit

for those people who no longer know them
those things those words
will be new to them
next year

nothing is visible
beyond next year
but one more year beyond that
things are much clearer
at this timeless spot
this is my tomorrow

today's things will never exist
beyond this moment
and the day after tomorrow
will have to be saved from tomorrow

एक दूसरा रास्ता

पचास दिन पहले जो एक अण्डा थी
अचानक मेरे सिर पर मँडरा गयी
यहाँ ज़रूर कोई घोंसला है

उसका एक दिन
मेरे दिन में से उड़कर
चला गया

उड़ान
तार की तरह झनझना रही है
जिस पर मैं अपने कपड़े तक
सुखा सकता हूँ

टहनी की तरह निकलकर
एक नहर
किसी दिन बंजर की ओर
बढ़ सकती है
नदी को नहीं मालूम
अगर मैं यहाँ टिक जाऊँ
तो समुद्र के अलावा
एक दूसरा रास्ता भी है

अगर मैं टिक जाऊँ
तो चिड़िया और जानवर
दोनों यहाँ रहना पसंद करेंगे
पत्तियों के पास
भूख भड़कानेवाली गन्ध है

कोई जानवर होता तो पता चलता
इन पत्तियों के पास
कितना स्वाद और कितनी खुराक है ?

Another Road

what fifty days ago was an egg
is now flying around my head
a nest must be nearby

once its day
flew from my day
and departed

the flight
is vibrating like a wire
where
I can also dry my clothes

one day
a canal will appear like a branch
it might turn
in the direction of the wasteland
the river doesn't know
should I stop here
or is there another road
than the one
leading to the sea

if I stop here
will the birds and the animals
be happy to live here
near the leaves
there is a smell that whets the appetite

if there were an animal here would it know
how much pleasure and food awaits
near these leaves

इस एकान्त में भड़की हुई
सपरिवार यादें
मन को सराय बना रही हैं
बच्चे और बच्चों के रिश्ते
मुझे कील-से खरोंच रहे हैं
किसी भी समय मेरे फेफड़ों की हवा
निकल सकती है ।

in this solitude
suddenly memories of my family
gather in my mind
kids and being around kids
like nails being driven into me
at any moment the air in my lungs
might give way

Notes

Introduction
The Introduction quotes from two interviews with Jagoori, both available on YouTube—Jasleen Vohra, "Āj Savere: An Interview with Leeladhar Jagoori" (*Doordarshan National*, September 17, 2015) and Anjum Sharma, "Leeladhar Jagudi on Hindi Poetry, Award Politics & Kedarnath" (*Sangat*, Ep. 9, *Hindwi.org*, February 24, 2023)—and the author's introductory essay, titled "The Lives of Old Desires" [purāne prasãg ke prāṇ], to a republication of his 1974 book *On This Journey* [is yātrā mẽ] (New Delhi: Rajkamal Prakashan, 2009).

"Things Begin Here"
In Hindu cosmology, the year of a god is 12,000 human years.

"The Bird's Birth"
In this volume, Jagoori never refers to a mother figure by the formal word "mātā." Instead, he uses "mã." This can be translated either by "mom," which I do most frequently, or "ma," as in this poem. *Ma* has a resonance that "mom" does not have. *Ma* speaks to the geographical-environmental-spiritual aspect of Hindu cosmology. This conjunction can be observed perhaps most clearly in how the Ganges River is called Ganga Ma, or Mother Ganges. This aspect of spiritual-environmental conjunction is important to Jagoori and to this poem in particular.

"Baldev Kathik"
This narrative poem centers on two fictional characters: Rangtu, a poor mountain villager arrested for stealing rations; and Baldev Kathik, the poem's title character, a subaltern police officer who comes into contact with Rangtu. In the poem's allegory, both are symbols of state-sponsored, police-enforced oppression.

Acknowledgments

Thanks to Ana Hontanilla Calatayud and Rose Facchini at *International Poetry Review*, the editorial staff at *Exchanges*, and Lauren Wolfe and Tuhin Bhattacharjee at *Barricade* for publishing some of these translations. Thanks as well to Matvei Yankelevich, Roz Naimi, Jake Syersak, and Henry Gifford for their editing.

Leeladhar Jagoori (b. 1940) is one of the leading Hindi poets in India. For his poetry, he has won the top literary and cultural awards in India, including the Sahitya Akademi Hindi Prize (1997); the Padma Shri (2004), a lifetime achievement award; and the KK Birla Foundation's Vyas Samman (2018), honoring excellence in the arts. He lives in Dehradun, Uttarakhand.

Matt Reeck has received fellowships for translation from the Guggenheim Foundation, the National Endowment for the Arts, and PEN. He won the 2020 Albertine Translation Prize for Zahia Rahmani's *"Muslim": A Novel*, and the 2022 Northwestern University Global Humanities Translation Prize for Abdelkébir Khatibi's *The Wound of the Name*. He translates from French, Hindi, Korean, and Urdu. He lives in Brooklyn with his family.

This book was typeset in Skolar, a contemporary serif designed by David Březina and Vaibhav Singh for Rosetta. Andrew Bourne designed the cover based on Chand Chaudhury's (चांद चौधरी) design of the original edition. Typesetting by Don't Look Now. Printed and bound by BALTO Print in Lithuania.

Marie-Noëlle Agniau
The Escapades
tr. Jesse Hover Amar

Jean-Paul Auxeméry
Selected Poems
tr. Nathaniel Tarn

Boethius
*The Poems from On the Consolation
of Philosophy*
tr. Peter Glassgold

Maria Borio
Transparencies
tr. Danielle Pieratti

Jeannette L. Clariond
Goddesses of Water
tr. Samantha Schnee

Jacques Darras
John Scotus Eriugena at Laon
tr. Richard Sieburth

Mario dell'Arco
Day Lasts Forever: Selected Poems
tr. Marc Alan Di Martino

Olivia Elias
Chaos, Crossing
tr. Kareem James Abu-Zeid

Jerzy Ficowski
Everything I Don't Know
tr. Jennifer Grotz & Piotr Sommer
PEN AWARD FOR POETRY IN TRANSLATION

Antonio Gamoneda
Book of the Cold
tr. Katherine M. Hedeen &
Víctor Rodríguez Núñez

Mireille Gansel
Soul House
tr. Joan Seliger Sidney

Óscar García Sierra
Houston, I'm the problem
tr. Carmen Yus Quintero

Phoebe Giannisi
Homerica
tr. Brian Sneeden

Zuzanna Ginczanka
On Centaurs & Other Poems
tr. Alex Braslavsky

Julien Gracq
Abounding Freedom
tr. Alice Yang

Leeladhar Jagoori
What of the Earth Was Saved
tr. Matt Reeck

*Nakedness Is My End:
Poems from the Greek Anthology*
tr. Edmund Keeley

Jazra Khaleed
The Light That Burns Us
ed. Karen Van Dyck

Judith Kiros
O
tr. Kira Josefsson

Dimitra Kotoula
The Slow Horizon That Breathes
tr. Maria Nazos

Maria Laina
Hers
tr. Karen Van Dyck

Maria Laina
Rose Fear
tr. Sarah McCann

Perrin Langda
A Few Microseconds on Earth
tr. Pauline Levy Valensi

Afrizal Malna
Document Shredding Museum
tr. Daniel Owen

Joyce Mansour
In the Glittering Maw: Selected Poems
tr. C. Francis Fisher

Manuel Maples Arce
Stridentist Poems
tr. KM Cascia

Ennio Moltedo
Night
tr. Marguerite Feitlowitz

Meret Oppenheim
The Loveliest Vowel Empties:
Collected Poems
tr. Kathleen Heil

Giovanni Pascoli
Last Dream
tr. Geoffrey Brock
RAIZISS/DE PALCHI TRANSLATION AWARD

Gabriel Pomerand
Saint Ghetto of the Loans
tr. Michael Kasper &
Bhamati Viswanathan

Rainer Maria Rilke
Where the Paths Do Not Go
tr. Burton Pike

Elisabeth Rynell
Night Talks
tr. Rika Lesser

Waly Salomão
Border Fare
tr. Maryam Monalisa Gharavi

George Sarantaris
Abyss and Song: Selected Poems
tr. Pria Louka

George Seferis
Book of Exercises II
tr. Jennifer R. Kellogg

Seo Jung Hak
The Cheapest France in Town
tr. Megan Sungyoon

Ardengo Soffici
Simultaneities & Lyric Chemisms
tr. Olivia E. Sears

Paul Verlaine
Before Wisdom: The Early Poems
tr. Keith Waldrop & K.A. Hays

Witold Wirpsza
Apotheosis of Music
tr. Frank L. Vigoda

Uljana Wolf
kochanie, today i bought bread
tr. Greg Nissan

Ye Lijun
My Mountain Country
tr. Fiona Sze-Lorrain

Verónica Zondek
Cold Fire
tr. Katherine Silver